Operation Rolling Thunder

Revised Edition

a proven 24/7 prayer strategy mobilizing the
Church and transforming cities

Tim Taylor

Contents

Endorsements

As I survey the hand of God moving across our nation, Washington State consistently rises up as one of the scenes of powerful divine action. A key to this has been the energetic work of Tim Taylor, a forerunner who has penetrated the state with a dynamic 24/7 transformational prayer movement. As you read about it in this book, you will catch the excitement and begin to burn with God's fire for reformation!

C. Peter Wagner

Chancellor Wagner Leadership Institute

Tim Taylor's book, *Operation Rolling Thunder*, is an excellent book on building prayer and worship into the fabric of a church, area, region or nation. Tim has lived and modeled these principles in front of my eyes and they work! Anyone who would like to see the rebuilding of the Lord's house into a house of prayer for all nations will want to read this! Tim builds this book on tested biblical principles and his military background. It is a privilege to be Tim's brother and friend.

Dan Hammer

Pastor Sonrise Chapel and Leader of the Northwest New Wine Network

Everett, Washington

Tim served as the Washington State Coordinator through this Task Force for several years. Through him, the Lord greatly expanded the on-going powerful place of prayer in Washington, and presently extends to other states and international cultures. Based on Biblical principles used intentionally by the military, Tim's background has led to prayer mobilization strategies that are greatly multiplying prayer covering in these mighty days. To God be the glory!

Lisa Crump

Director of Prayer Mobilization

National Day of Prayer Task Force

May we discover that our Father is a reformer, His son is a reformer and the Holy Spirit is a reformer! Together they are dissatisfied with the state of current affairs and committed to reform. They will not rest until their plans are completed, nor should we. God is on the move, with or without us. The question before each of us is; Do we have the courage to join in His Kingdom Reformation. The work you now hold in your hands is all about reformation. It is an aid to connect the passion of God with your personal destiny.

Jake Dragseth

Pastor New Song Foursquare Church

Port Townsend, Washington

I have known Tim Taylor for many years, working closely with him while the material in this book was being developed. I believe the Lord has given Tim an apostolic blueprint to unite the Church in the common cause of revival through networking the intercessors throughout the state (and ultimately the nation) in a harmonious, Holy Spirit orchestrated cry to Him. Many leaders are looking for the type of information that God has already given Tim. Look no further!

Joe McIntyre

President, International Fellowship of Ministries

Bothell, Washington

With his military background, Tim has been inspired by our Lord Jesus and given a strategy for divine change. He has been given the vision for taking our cities and states for God. He has chronicled this movement in this book.

Kirk Pearson

Washington State Representative, 39th District

It has been said "Thunder is justified after lightening has struck." Manifestations of power are to be more than just noise. *Operation Rolling Thunder* details the account of an apostolic strategy to touch a region and change the hearts of men as the lightening of God's truth is confirmed with signs following. Tim's book is powerful testimony of what can happen when God's people pray, take Him at His Word, act on it in obedience and then worship and praise The Lord of Host as He routs the enemy for the souls of men.

Greg J Daley

Associate pastor Seattle Revival Center
Vice president of International Fellowship of Ministries

If you are looking for real life examples of what God will do with people take a look at this book. Tim has done an outstanding work at not only presenting the work of apostolic gifting, but in cataloging the series of events that took place in Washington State as a result of Operation Rolling Thunder, a prayer movement that swept across our state and is still moving into its strategic place in a worldwide awakening. Tim brings to life and puts sinew on the gifts God has given across the body and makes it easy for anyone to apply the meaning of apostolic, prophetic to real life.

Gail Homan

Senior Pastor, .Seattle Revival Center New Castle, Washington

Some things men endorse and then there are those things sent to us from the Lord. I meet many men and women of God in my travels as a teacher in Body of Christ. Tim Taylor is one of those men who are real. His heart is sincerely after the Lord and he is one the Lord trusts with Kingdom work. It is obvious his writings and ministry are from the Lord. Tim and Brenda have become like my own children to me and I heartily recommend his ministry and this book to you.

Donald W. Dodd

Apostle~ Freedom in Christ Ministries, North Pole, Alaska

"Tim Taylor is a man of proven character exhibited by his discipline and holy walk before the Lord. Therefore, he has been entrusted by the Lord Himself to teach the Body of Christ the dynamics of penetrating prayer and spiritual warfare. It is my hope that this insightful book will be studied by ministers, students, and Christian workers everywhere. It is a "must read" for those serious about the establishment of the Kingdom of God in their communities."

Dr. Flo Ellers

Glory Global Ministries

Aberdeen, Washington

I have known Tim Taylor for over a decade. He has been tenacious in pursuing and refining the vision of CONECT. This book is a practical application of these Biblical principles. I trust it will have a wide readership. It is an important text in doing Kingdom work.

The Rev'd. Dr. John Roddam

Rector, St. Luke's Episcopal Church

Seattle, Washington

Drawing from biblical patterns in the Word, and military experience gained in Desert Storm, Tim Taylor offers an effective strategy for connecting leaders and establishing 24/7 prayer in order to see cities and communities transformed. Using Washington State as a prototype, this book documents what can happen when the body of Christ comes together and prays in unity to see the Kingdom advance. You'll be encouraged by the practical tools as well as the broad vision Tim shares that will enable you to impact your world.

Diane M. Fink

Educational Resource Director, Aglow International

Edmonds, Washington

I would like to highly recommend "Operation Rolling Thunder" as a dramatic testimony of what happens when Christians join together for a common purpose. Tim Taylor proves God is a "Man Of War" and very ready in this season to honor the biblical promises of unity where, "One will put a thousand to flight and two, ten thousand." As a graduate of the United States Naval War College Strategies Course, Tim takes us through a Spiritual War College with a testimony that will help anyone graduate--Anchors Away!

Al Houghton

Founder of Word at Work Ministries and Author

Placentia, California

This book is dedicated to my Lord and Savior, Jesus Christ, the King of Glory and the Lord of hosts.

Without the help of my bride, Brenda, this work would have not been completed for your bride, the Church.

FOREWORD

God does dynamic things through dynamic individuals. Dynamic individuals are people who step out in faith and dare to dream and dare to achieve for the purpose of God's kingdom reign. Tim Taylor is one of those dynamic individuals. His desire is to find other like-minded forerunners who want to achieve God's dynamic purpose for the Church and cities, and thus, their own dynamic destiny. He has been anointed and appointed by God for this assignment: to mobilize spiritual forerunners for the Army of God.

Taylor has been referred to as a John the Baptist-type preacher (prophetic and apostolic); similar to Apostle Peter's personality type; and a pioneer-type like Jeremiah Johnson. He has been both a corporate and military warrior strategist. Now he is a spiritual warfare strategist in the heavenlies. He brings down the thunder and rain of God to city problems, conflicts, and crisis. His insightful teachings presented in this book, and in seminars, will open the mind, eyes, and heart, as it did mine, to the awesome majesty and power of God to intervene in the affairs of a city.

Operation Rolling Thunder II is a clarion call for intercessors and prophetic people to come together for a divine power encounter and to open up the heavenlies for   God to pour down a blessing over each one's assignment for transformation, which will affect every sphere of influence.

Now get ready, get reading, and get going on this divine journey!

Dr. John P. Kelly
CEO, LEAD
(Leadership Education for Advancement and Development)
CEO, ICWBF
(International Christian WealthBuilders Foundation)
Presiding Apostle, ICA (International Coalition of Apostles)

Chapter 1

Introduction

This book contains the story of the 24/7 transformational prayer movement linking with the emerging apostolic networks flowing out of Washington State. When Brenda and I were called into the ministry in the early 90's, our vision was "to declare and prepare." This book will follow that pattern. It declares revelation from scripture; - how that revelation has been applied today; the corresponding signs and wonders God gave in response, along with lessons learned to prepare others to apply the biblical pattern in their city and region. It will equip churches throughout the world with a strategy to mobilize and sustain 24/7 prayer, while simultaneously connecting the elders of a city or region quickly. This strategy links the 24/7 prayer movement with leaders from the seven spheres of society to enact a long term campaign to transform their region through the gospel of Jesus Christ.

Are You A Forerunner?

In 2007 I received a call from a reporter at the Christian Examiner. She began her interview by saying, "Tim, I am an Evangelical from this mainline denomination and you scare me. You remind me of John the Baptist or   Jeremiah Johnson." I had to laugh. Actually that was a pretty accurate description because John the Baptist was a forerunner and Jeremiah Johnson was a pioneer and a mountain man. I've known for years that I was a forerunner and a pioneer, seeing things that others do not, and being willing to share what I see; wanting to explore new territory. However, I had never considered the description of a mountain man until the reporter mentioned Jeremiah Johnson.

It is true. I am a mountain man. I am a man who is passionate about Mount Zion, the mountain of the Lord where David's tabernacle was located.

Hebrews 6:20 tells us that Jesus was a forerunner. He saw things afar off and He shared what He saw with His disciples. He lived with them, taught them, and demonstrated His vision. Yet sometimes they still did not understand what He was trying to communicate. In Matthew 16, Jesus tells his disciples to beware of the leaven of the Pharisees. They figured it was because they did not bring any bread. They heard with their ears but they failed to perceive with their hearts. They did not understand. When Jesus became aware of their perception he said:

> *Matthew 16:9-12 Do you not yet understand, or remember the five loaves of the five thousand and how many baskets you took up? Nor the seven loaves of the four thousand and how many large baskets you took up? How is it you do not understand that I did not speak to you concerning bread? — but to beware of the leaven of the Pharisees and Sadducees." Then they understood that He did not tell them to beware of the leaven of bread, but of the doctrine of the Pharisees and Sadducees.*

Jesus saw something that took His disciples just a little longer to catch. What was obvious to Him was a mystery to them. It sounds to me like Jesus might have been a little frustrated. Yet God has provided forerunners as a gift. In Isaiah 49, the prophecy speaks about Jesus, the servant who will be a light to the Gentiles:

Isaiah 49:4   Then I said, 'I have labored in vain, I have spent my strength for nothing and in vain; Yet surely my just reward is with the Lord, And my work with my God.'''

It is important to remember that the work and reward of forerunners are with our God. Dutch Sheets says in the foreword to "The Forerunner Anointing" by Dr. Eddie Lawrence:

"I realized, in fact, that God was often allowing me to see things before He began the process of revealing them to others. This didn't make me privileged, and certainly not more spiritual. It was simply that God intended for me to be apart of the revealing process – one of the forerunners through whom new directions and mindsets would be revealed."

Forerunners have to be careful to guard their hearts and minds. Otherwise, hurts and wounds can result. I have learned that, wounded people wound people and frustrated people can frustrate people. Thank God that there are ministers and ministries (e.g. Shiloh Place, Restoring the Foundation, Elijah House, etc.) who are called to serve wounded people.

Often pastors can have   conflict with forerunners and people with a prophetic gifting in their congregations. The forerunner can get frustrated because seemingly no action is taken, while the pastor is frustrated because the forerunner seems not to consider the present condition of the flock. Forerunners are always looking afar off, declaring what they see coming around the bend. Sometimes the forerunner's message is not clear because either the message is poorly communicated or the hearer's hearts are not prepared to perceive. Other times the forerunner gives the message to the wrong audience. I have made all of these mistakes. Thank God He has made provision to build what the forerunners declare through the apostolic anointing.

How many of you have seen things God wants to do in your church and your city? You just know that God wants to establish 24/7 prayer, praise and worship. You are passionate about uniting the body of Christ in your city and region? You know God wants to draw together strategic leaders like apostles, prophets, government leaders and business leaders in your city. You are certain God is mobilizing an army to reach out into all spheres of society in order to transform it. You cried out, you labored, you worked, but it seemed in vain. It seemed like no one, or very few, understood.

Well, join the crowd of forerunners! That is right, I said crowd. Forerunners are located in every church, every city and every region. Some of you are called intercessor; some are called watchmen or prophets; others are called net-workers; some are called apostles and many are called crazy, which is simply another word for passionate. I do not want to get into a theological discussion about apostles and prophets now. However, I do want to talk about function. Forerunners carry a prophetic and an apostolic anointing. Both anointings are needed. There are   many of you crying out because:

Amos 3:7 Surely the Lord God does nothing, unless He reveals His secret to His servants the prophets.

Forerunners are Strategically Placed by God

Strategic placement is one of the reasons that there are so many of you. Yet you can also feel alone. God has strategically placed people who carry prophetic and apostolic anointings in many local churches, cities and regions. The role of the prophetic is to declare what is coming, and the role of the apostolic is to build that which the prophetic people declare. In order to receive the benefit of these gifts they - need to be both recognized and honored.

Matthew 10:41 He who receives a prophet in the name of a prophet shall receive a prophet's reward. And he who receives a righteous man in the name of a righteous man shall receive a righteous man's reward.

Now, back to the interview; the reason I was being interviewed by the Christian Examiner was that I was the State Coordinator for the National Day of Prayer. I also spearheaded Operation Rolling Thunder. ORT is a 24/7 prayer strategy linking National Day of Prayer, Prayer Week and the Global Day of Prayer events with the 24/7 transformational prayer movement and the emerging city and regional apostolic networks. As the reporter ended the interview, I said "If you would like, I can introduce you to a number of other coordinators and CONECTers across our state who you could interview to finish your article." A CONECTer is someone who has been trained in our Christian Outreach Network Establishing City-wide Teamwork program. I   shared that our coordinator in

Yakima attended a Catholic church; the CONECTer in Olympia attended a Messianic church. The list went on to include coordinators and CONECTers who were Nazarene, Methodist, Baptist, Apostolic, Pentecostal, Assembly of God, Episcopal, Charismatic, independent and more. All these were forerunners strategically placed by God all across our state; and they represented almost every stream.

While I will share with you some dramatic things God has done in these last three years, I fully realize that what has been accomplished is only because of the people who have been faithful to pray, prophesy and act for years. Their ceiling provided my foundation. Vivian is a perfect example. I had the honor of meeting a great forerunner, Vivian, in Whatcom County just before she went home to be with our Lord. She was over 90 years old, and she had been faithful to intercede for more than six decades. Vivian was just beginning to see things manifest that she had prayed for over many years. Vivian is relatively unknown here on earth, but I know she is well known in heaven. I know there are so many Vivians out there.

Our CONECTer in Whatcom County, Pastor Jason Hubbard, has done an awesome job mobilizing the body of Christ there and the fruit of his ministry has contributed to some impressive church growth. In addition, I would be remiss if I did not mention all of the faithful pastors, ministers, apostles, prophets, teachers, evangelists, watchmen, intercessors and prayer coordinators who have taken the lead in their areas. Without each person and ministry doing their part, there would be no testimony for our Lord Jesus. This is certainly not the work of one person. However, I have done and will do my part. If I do my job right, it is my hope and expectation that my ceiling will become another's foundation. I thank God and honor all of those, known and unknown, who have played a part in God's unfolding plan.

So if you are one of those frustrated forerunners who are passionate about:

- Establishing 24/7 prayer in your city
- Drawing together the elders of your city
- Transformation that affects the seven spheres of society
- Uniting the body of Christ
- The emerging city and regional apostolic networks

Then for all you do, this book is for you!

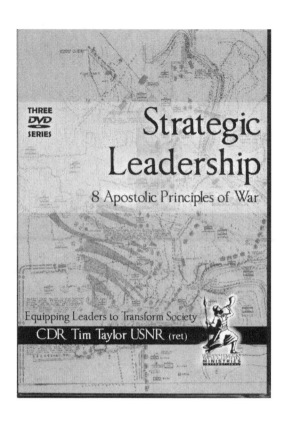

THREE DVD SERIES

Strategic Leadership
8 Apostolic Principles of War

Equipping Leaders to Transform Society
CDR Tim Taylor USNR (ret)

This powerful five hour training series is available at
www.ORTPrayer.org and www.KingdomLeague.org

CHAPTER 2

The Restoration of David's Tabernacle

I have learned through the years that God uses patterns. Patterns provide a blue print or a diagram so that what was built once can be built again. The bible also teaches us that the Old Testament was a type and shadow, or a pattern, of the New Testament. Jesus was sent to proclaim the gospel of the kingdom. King David provides the best example of the kingdom in the Old Testament. He began by gathering all the leaders in a city who had a passion to set one person in as king. The very next step was to bring back the presence of God. This was done in the city of David on MT Zion through continual prayer, praise and worship.

The purpose of this book is to share with you the pattern that God showed me to apply through Operation Rolling Thunder and CONECT. The intention is to empower everyone with a passion to see Jesus set as the king over their city and to provide a practical way to apply the same pattern David did. To understand David's tabernacle we need to begin with Moses.

God showed Moses how to build His tabernacle and commanded Him to make everything according to the pattern He gave him. God also gave King David plans for Solomon's temple.

Exodus 25:9 According to all that I show you, that is, the pattern of the tabernacle and the pattern of all its furnishings, just so you shall make it.

1 Chronicles 28:11-12 Then David gave his son Solomon the plans for the vestibule, its houses, its treasuries, its upper chambers, its inner chambers, and the place of the mercy seat; 12 and the plans for all that he had by the Spirit, of the courts of the house of the Lord, of all the chambers all around, of the treasuries of the house of God, and of the treasuries for the dedicated things...

Patterns

The word translated as "pattern" in Exodus 25:9 and as "plans" in 1 Chronicles 28:11 is the same Hebrew word - "tabniyth." It means model, plan, structure or pattern. Because the Old Testament is a pattern for the New Testament, whenever I look at the Old Testament, I look for patterns.

Romans 15:4 says that "whatever things were written before were written for our learning, that we through the patience and comfort of the Scriptures might have hope."

A pattern provides certain keys that enable others to imitate or model the original design. In Mathew 16:19, Jesus says that He will give us keys to the kingdom. In the following chapters, I will declare to you the pattern God revealed to me, as well as the results of applying this pattern through Operation Rolling Thunder. It is my hope and prayer that you will thus be prepared to apply the pattern to transform your church, your city, your region and beyond.

God Spoke Through Operation Desert Storm

In order to help you understand what I see, I need to share with you my experience in Operation Desert Storm. In 1991, I was recalled from the Navy Reserve to serve as a Naval Liaison Officer. During my tour of duty, I spent part of my time serving on the staff of Rear Admiral Taylor, Commander of U.S. Naval Forces, Central Command aboard the USS La Salle. Rear Admiral Taylor was responsible for all naval forces in that theater of operations. In essence, we ran the war for the Navy. This is important because it provided a frame work for God to speak to me.

Operation Desert Storm was launched because the little country of Kuwait had been overrun by Iraq, and the population was being held captive by the enemy army. The people were oppressed. They wanted to be liberated. In Desert Storm, a coalition air force of 38 nations came together to bomb an enemy into submission. There were reports that, due to changes in the weather just prior to the invasion, land mines had been exposed. There are numerous individual testimonies of God's intervention which saved people's lives. In fact, I am convinced at one point that an angel intervened upon my behalf and saved my life. But that is a story for another time.

The air campaign was very effective; so much so that when our ground forces went forth, we saw a victory of biblical proportions. There were so many Iraqi soldiers surrendering that our forces were overwhelmed. In fact, some of the Iraqi's came out thanking us for capturing them. Jeremiah 50 and 51 came alive to me knowing that Iraq was the location of Babylon .

Then the Lord spoke to me saying, "First the natural and then the spiritual." This was a   reminder to me about patterns.

Before I go on, I need to make something very clear. Throughout this book you will find references to the army, war, battles etc.. However, scripture is clear in 2 Corinthians 10 and Ephesians 6 that our war is not with flesh and blood. Our fight is with spiritual armies of wickedness in heavenly places. The strongholds referred to are twisted ways of thinking that allow demonic forces to hold people's minds captive. Romans 12:21 teaches us to overcome evil with good. The Church's responsibility is to represent Jesus on this earth to mankind. Romans chapter 13 teaches us that God ordained governments to deal with civil disobedience and to provide justice. So all references to war, warfare, battles, armies etc. are spiritual references. The natural references point to the spiritual reality.

In Desert Storm, as I mentioned earlier, we saw a victory of biblical proportions. In these last days, God is raising up a coalition prayer force that will bomb the enemy into submission. Then, when spiritual ground forces (leaders in all 7 spheres, outreach, ministry, etc.) go forth, we will see a victory of biblical proportions. People who were held captive by sin will be set free.

In the '90s God raised up movements, such as "March for Jesus" and "Praying through the 10/40 Window." These movements mobilized the most massive coordinated efforts to date, and they have not ended. They have only continued to grow through new events.

God is a Man of War Mobilizing an Army

Starting in 1991 through 1993 God began to speak to me about combining the restoration of David's tabernacle, the 24/7 prayer movement, and the mobilization of the army of the Lord. I foresaw the day when the body of Christ would be linked together, but not based upon denominational lines. This coalition would be united in a geographic area around a common objective to transform a specific city. I knew that the army of the Lord would face the in the spiritual realm the same challenges that the Army, Navy, Air Force, Marines, Coast Guard, and coalition forces faced in the natural.

After a season of studying the name of God as Lord of Hosts, I received revelation regarding my responsibility to prepare for this time of coalition. Part of my preparation was to study scripture and ask the Lord questions. The Holy Spirit started by emphasizing a revelation of God's name. God is called Yahweh Tsabaoth (Lord of Hosts, or Lord of the Armies) over 245 times in the word of God. That is almost two and a half times more than any of the other Jehovah names. He is the ultimate admiral and general.

Exodus 15:3 The Lord is a man of war; The Lord is His name.

As a Naval Officer I studied the principles of war. These principles have been taught for over 2,500 years and the reason they are still taught is that they work. Each of the major principles of war works because they are biblically based. (For an in depth study, get the book Developing Apostolic Strategy from www.ORTPrayer.org & www.KingdomLeague.org).

In Ezekiel 37:1-10, the prophet prophesied to the dry bones. These bones came together bone to bone and joint to joint then flesh and skin covered them.

Ezekiel 37:10 So I prophesied as He commanded me, and breath came into them, and they lived, and stood upon their feet, an exceedingly great army.

This is a pattern for our time. God is now raising up an exceedingly great and mighty spiritual army. I learned in the Navy War College that armies exist to project power in order to enforce the will of their governments. Therefore, the army of the Lord exists to project power to enforce the will of King Jesus.

To learn more about how the army of the Lord should be mobilized and deployed, I looked to the Old Testament as it provides us types and shadows of what is to come. I also looked to see if there were any prophetic declarations that refer to the time we live in today.

Restoring David's Tabernacle

God is a man of war and He is raising up an army today because He intends to restore a previous tabernacle that captured His heart.

> *Acts 15:16-17 "After this I will return And will rebuild the tabernacle of David, which has fallen down; I will rebuild its ruins, And I will set it up; So that the rest of mankind may seek the Lord, Even all the Gentiles who are called by My name, Says the Lord who does all these things." (See also Amos 9:11-12)*

This leads us to the question: where was the Tabernacle of David located? The Tabernacle of David was located on Mount Zion in the city of David. The first thing David did after he was made king over all Israel was to consult with elders and military leaders about bringing back the presence of God, which was resident in the Ark of the Covenant. He wanted to have the presence of God with him in his city, so he set up a tent on Zion and placed the Ark of the Covenant in it. *I believe that, by studying what King David did, we can discover keys to help us bring the presence of God to any city.*

King David was a man after God's own heart. He was a psalmist and a worshipper. He was also a warrior and led troops into battle. He became a wise military commander. In 1 Chronicles 11, David gathered with the military leaders and the elders at Hebron. The Strong's Concordance says that Hebron means "seat of association." Dictionary.com says that association means "an organization of people with a common purpose having a formal structure." It also means friendship, companionship or place of connection. So all the leaders in Israel came together and connected with a common purpose - to make one king. In these last days, God is calling His leaders to connect with a common purpose. That purpose is to make one king, and that king is Jesus. We will do this through the establishment of the gospel of the kingdom.

Matthew 4:23 And Jesus went about all Galilee, teaching in their synagogues, preaching the gospel of the kingdom , and healing all kinds of sickness and all kinds of disease among the people.

Matthew 24:14 And this gospel of the kingdom will be preached in all the world as a witness to all the nations, and then the end will come.

In Matthew 6:9-12, Jesus also taught us to pray that His kingdom would come on earth as it was in heaven. It was in light of these scriptures regarding the kingdom that I began to study King David and his kingdom. I wanted to see what I could learn since the kingdom expanded further under David's reign than under any other king.

Moses instituted offerings and David added praise and worship to the offerings to bring back the presence of God. In 2 Samuel 6, 1 Chronicles 16 and 1 Chronicles 23-25 we see how David accomplished this. He began with a procession of praise and worship that included harps, stringed instruments, tambourines, cymbals, shouting, dancing, and offerings. It was an extravagant celebration of praise and worship.

David then went to great effort in order to ensure that continual prayer, praise and worship was offered up on MT Zion. He appointed Levitical teams of singers and musicians who prophesied, prayed, praised and worshiped the Lord continually.

To summarize, the first thing David did to establish his kingdom was to gather the appointed leaders and consult with them regarding bringing back the presence of the Lord. Then extravagant praise and worship went with the presence of God into the City of David up to Mount Zion.

Psalm 22:3 But You are holy, Enthroned in the praises of Israel.

Zion is the place where continual 24/7 prayer praise and worship was offered up. God loves Zion, where His praises reside. He longs for the restoration of this pattern of a tabernacle today.

Psalm 76:2 In Salem also is His tabernacle, And His dwelling place in Zion.

Psalm 132:13 For the Lord has chosen Zion; He has desired it for His dwelling place...

Joel 3:17 "So you shall know that I am the Lord your God, Dwelling in Zion My holy mountain..."

What have we learned about the pattern?

- God is a man of war and the Lord of the armies of heaven. Understanding His name as Lord of the Hosts helps us understand aspects of His character, nature and wisdom which we can apply to mobilizing the body of Christ to transform cities. I strongly believe this revelation will radically change how the Church functions together corporately.

- God is raising up a spiritual army to enforce the will of King Jesus. War in this book is in a spiritual sense because our warfare is not against people, but against spiritual hosts of wickedness.

- Just as David's first step to build the kingdom was to gather the leaders in a city with the goal to make one king, our goal today is to make Jesus Lord King in every city. This is accomplished through the presentation of the gospel.

- Our second step is to follow King David's pattern by establishing 24/7 prayer, praise and worship in a city just as he did on Mount Zion with the tabernacle he set up in the City of David.

Questions

1. Are the elders of your city being gathered together on a regular basis to pray? Who are they? How can you connect with them?

2. Are Christian leaders representing the church, business, government, media, education, healthcare and the family being represented in the gathering of elders? What can you do to include them and foster their success?

3. Are there any churches or ministries in your city who are working on a vision to establish 24/7 prayer?? Who are they? How can you support their efforts?

Chapter 3

THE POWER OF PRAYER, PRAISE AND WORSHIP

Remember, the tabernacle of David, the man of worship, was located in Zion. God desires Zion as His dwelling place. David established as a pattern a place where singers and musicians prophesied, prayed, praised and worshiped the Lord continually.

When I think of King David, the leader over the armies of Israel, I cannot help but think of my experience in the military. One of the things you desire when you go to war is air supremacy. It makes the job of the ground forces much easier if the heaven above is clear of the enemy. Following David's pattern, hte priests who interceded, prayed, sang and prophesied were like David's air force. Their prayer, praise and worship provided a place where power was projected in support of ground forces.

> *Isaiah 4:5-6 …then the Lord will create above every dwelling place of Mount Zion, and above her assemblies, a cloud and smoke by day and the shining of a flaming fire by night. For over all the glory there will be a covering. And there will be a tabernacle for shade in the daytime from the heat, for a place of refuge, and for a shelter from storm and rain.*

31

Psalm 2:6-9 "Yet I have set My King on My holy hill of Zion. I will declare the decree: The Lord has said to Me, 'You are My Son, Today I have begotten You. Ask of Me, and I will give You the nations for Your inheritance, and the ends of the earth for Your possession. You shall break them with a rod of iron; You shall dash them to pieces like a potter's vessel.'"

Psalm 110:2 The Lord shall send the rod of Your strength out of Zion. Rule in the midst of Your enemies!

Judah means praise in Hebrew, and Genesis 49:10 says that the ruler's staff, or scepter, will never depart from Judah. So we understand that praise and rule are connected. In Psalm 149 we see that praise and abandoned worship with instruments and dance are very powerful. From a place of praise, righteous decrees shall be made as a people hear the voice of the Lord and release His word upon this earth.

Psalm 149:6-9 Let the high praises of God be in their mouth, And a two-edged sword in their hand, To execute vengeance on the nations, And punishments on the peoples; To bind their kings with chains, And their nobles with fetters of iron; To execute on them the written judgment — This honor have all His saints.

Can you imagine how powerful it was for David's kingdom to have this kind of prayer coverage available to them? This prayer was like his air force clearing the air so that his ground forces could move forward unobstructed. Today, this kind of continual prayer helps open the heavens over a city so that wisdom and revelation from God's throne - with answers in the spheres of business, healthcare, education, the media, etc. - will all come more easily.

It is the god of this age who blinds the eyes and stops the ears of unbelievers so that they cannot see or hear the good news. As we mobilize intercessors, watchmen, singers, and musicians in cities to be like the Air Force (aim high, join the prayer force), they provide a continual canopy of prayer cover over our cities. How much more effective will our ground forces, who present the gospel through outreach, ministry be?

In Mercy a Throne Is Set for Judgment

Psalm 22:3 says, "But You are holy, enthroned in the praises of Israel." The word "enthroned" is yashab in the Hebrew. It means to sit down (specifically as a judge, in ambush, in quiet), to dwell, to settle and to marry. As I meditated on this scripture I marveled at how multifaceted God is. For example, God is love and, at the same time, He is a consuming fire. His zeal can lead to great tenderness, kindness and affection, for His bride, the Church, , while simultaneously it can be very dangerous to an enemy who would attack His bride. Hence, God can serve as a judge ordering the ambush of an enemy, while simultaneously presiding over a marriage.

In essence, praise creates a big chair for God to come and sit as a judge, clearing the way for the pronouncement of the gospel. Daniel 7:9 says that Daniel watched until the thrones were put in place and the Ancient of Days was seated. Thrones are set for judgment. Daniel 7:22

goes on to describe how there was one making war against the saints of God and overcoming them:

> ...until the Ancient of Days came, and a judgment was made in favor of the saints of the Most High, and the time came for the saints to possess the kingdom.

Now is the time for the saints of God to possess the kingdom. A judgment will be rendered in favor of the saints. As I meditated on this, I remembered other scriptures that paint the picture of the courtroom, with a prosecutor, witnesses, testimony, a legal advocate and the judge. Satan is the accuser of the brethren, Jesus is our advocate, God the Father is the judge.

> Isaiah 43:25-26 I, even I, am He who blots out your transgressions for My own sake; And I will not remember your sins. Put Me in remembrance; Let us contend together; State your case, that you may be acquitted.

> Revelation 12:10-12 Then I heard a loud voice saying in heaven, "Now salvation, and strength, and the kingdom of our God, and the power of His Christ have come, for the accuser of our brethren, who accused them before our God day and night, has been cast down. And they overcame him by the blood of the Lamb and by the word of their testimony, and they did not love their lives to the death.

Isaiah 16:5 In mercy the throne will be established; And One will sit on it in truth, in the tabernacle of David, judging and seeking justice and hastening righteousness.

I like what Rick Joiner says in his book, <u>Epic Battles of the Last Days</u>. On page 20 he states, "the scriptures reveal that there are two acts which go on continually before the throne of God – intercession and accusation." He goes on to state that while Satan no longer is able to go before God's throne because he was thrown out of heaven, he uses the saints, who do have access to God's throne. Joiner says, "to the degree that the enemy has access to our lives he will use us to accuse and criticize the brethren." Which witness would you like to bring before God, accusation or intercession?

His throne is set for MERCY. Praise creates a throne for God to come and sit as a judge, but He desires to have audience with us that we may seek His deliverance from our enemy. To this end, He made provision for our sin through Jesus that we might be delivered from our adversary the Devil.

1 John 2:1 My little children, these things I write to you, so that you may not sin. And if anyone sins, we have an Advocate with the Father, Jesus Christ the righteous.

Isaiah 54:17 No weapon formed against you shall prosper, And every tongue which rises against you in judgment You shall condemn. This is the heritage of the servants of the Lord, And their righteousness is from Me," Says the Lord.

35

Hebrews 7:25 Therefore He is also able to save to the uttermost those who come to God through Him, since He always lives to make intercession for them.

When it comes time to render a decision, God speaks. He seeks those who would hear His word and then proclaim it on the earth, exercising His judgment.

Micah 4:2-3 Many nations shall come and say, "Come, and let us go up to the mountain of the Lord, To the house of the God of Jacob;He will teach us His ways, And we shall walk in His paths." For out of Zion the law shall go forth, And the word of the Lord from Jerusalem. He shall judge between many peoples, And rebuke strong nations afar off...

Isaiah 44:7 And who can proclaim as I do? Then let him declare it and set it in order for Me....

Psalm 68:11 The Lord gave the word;Great was the company of those who proclaimed it...

Hearing and proclaiming the judgments of God is key to establishing the gospel of the kingdom. God's people need to hear our Father's spoken word and then release that judgment on the earth.

King David was a man after God's own heart, yet he committed adultery and murder. According to the law, he should have been killed. But, when   confronted with his sin by Nathan the prophet, David was quick to repent. Because of his change of heart, David received the mercy of the Lord. Al Houghton, in his book The Sure Mercies of David pages 13-14, says:

> "As we approach the culmination of the ages, representing Jesus in the end-times is for the church an awesome and amazing assignment. In many ways, the church should be commended for displaying the heart and soul of Jesus in the gospels for many decades. Psalm 2 promises nations as an inheritance for a great end-time harvest, while Revelation outlines a variety and increase of judgments for those choosing to reject God and His ways. The challenge is for the church to walk in both worlds.
>
> The sure mercies of David bring an understanding which empowers both streams of Jesus' ministry. The covenantal care of "Sure Mercy" promises redemption for our failures by transforming them into a platform for our greatest success. As we gain proficiency at redeeming failure, God promises in Isaiah 55 that nations will run to us. Possessing nations promised in Psalm 2 demands a message of redemption – "Sure Mercy" is that message.
>
> The first edge of "Sure Mercy" brings covenantal redemption but the second strictly judgment. David understood covenant mercy meant judgment to the enemy. He specifically prayed, prophesied and proclaimed covenantal judgment in Psalms. We cannot display a heart like David without entering this realm. "Sure Mercy" is a two-edged sword!…. A church incapable of swinging a two-edged sword is a church unprepared to   accurately represent Jesus as

Savior and Judge….As in the Davidic pattern, the covenant of "Sure Mercy" invited outcasts to become "mighty men" who change nations."

Are you a forerunner like King David? In spite of his sins, God used him set a standard. His example should give us all hope. God has incredible love for us and He redeems failure.

Under David's administration the tabernacle of David was erected and the borders of the kingdom were expanded as he defeated enemies all around. This led to a reign of peace for his son, Solomon. God had given David the plans and provision to build a house for God. The next generation, during Solomon's reign, was prepared to build Solomon's Temple.

Are you a forerunner like David? Do you want God to use you as an example of His ability to redeem failure? Do you want to transform a city and a nation like David did? Then it is time to get equipped.

What keys have we learned about the Davidic pattern?

- Continual prayer, praise and worship provide a place of refuge and protection.
- Praise creates a place for God to sit as Judge. His throne is set for judgment and for mercy, so that saints can possess the kingdom.
- 24/7/365 prayer, praise and worship convenes the courtroom of heaven so that, as the Judge renders decisions, decrees can be made and power projected to set people free from bondage.

- God used King David as a pattern to show how His covenant of "sure mercy" brings both deliverance and judgment.

Visit www.ORTPrayer.org and get equipped to mobilize your church and city. Substantial discounts are available when you order 10 or more books.

Chapter 4

The Gospel of the Kingdom

I hope you have noticed by now a number of references to establishing the gospel of the kingdom. A whole book could easily be devoted to this subject. For now, I want to focus on just a few aspects of the kingdom as it pertains to a New Testament believer. John the Baptist and Jesus both began their ministry with this message: "… the kingdom of heaven is at hand." Jesus went on to say that the good news of the kingdom would be preached in every nation.

Matthew 24:14 And this gospel of the kingdom will be preached in all the world as a witness to all the nations, and then the end will come.

In a kingdom, a king rules! In this case, Jesus is the King. Our heavenly Father used David's kingdom as a pattern. He then sent Jesus who laid the foundation of the kingdom of God in the New Testament and set the best example for us all to follow. The book of Romans gives us a better picture of what the kingdom looks like to the New Testament believer.

41

Romans 14:17 for the kingdom of God is not eating and drinking, but righteousness and peace and joy in the Holy Spirit.

A key aspect in the kingdom is righteousness. Basically, it means "right" or "justice." Can a man do the right thing if his heart is not right? Jesus taught us that from the abundance of the heart the mouth speaks. Unrighteous thoughts proceed from an unrighteous heart. Actions follow thoughts. This can lead to sin. Isaiah 59:2 teaches us that sin cuts off our fellowship with God. Thanks be to God, who sent us His son Jesus to fulfill the righteous requirements of the law that we might have fellowship with Him.

One of the primary keys for success in David's kingdom was that he had regular fellowship with God. This fellowship with our heavenly Father caused his thinking to be righteous. His righteous thoughts led to the actions which established his kingdom.

When our hearts are right with God, we can commune with Him. As we commune with Him, our thoughts are changed. As our thoughts are changed, our actions are also affected. As we dwell on righteous thoughts, we tend to do right things. Peace and joy follow. As I sought for wisdom on how to apply this simple truth, the Lord reminded me of two things: the first was the message with which Jesus began His ministry, and the second was a proverb.

Matthew 4:17 From that time Jesus began to preach and to say, "Repent , for the kingdom of heaven is at hand."

Proverbs 29:2 When the righteous are in authority, the people rejoice;But when a wicked man rules, the people groan.

Jesus had a core message. It was, "Repent, or change your mind, for the kingdom of heaven is at hand." Then the Lord asked me a question. "What is that is in your hand?" What are you personally responsible for? The areas where you are responsible are the areas where you have authority. Those are the areas where you are responsible to establish the good news of the kingdom.

There is a wonderful principle about such responsibility found in Luke 19. It is the parable of the minas. A nobleman gave 10 servants 10 minas and said, "Do business till I come." When the nobleman returned, he had each servant give an account of what he entrusted to them.

Luke 19:17 And he said to him, 'Well done, good servant; because you were faithful in a very little, have authority over ten cities.'

If you are faithful in little, God will entrust you with more. The key to establishing the gospel begins with taking personal responsibility to establish the gospel of the kingdom in your own life.. **You cannot lead others where you do not go yourself.** What will it take to make things right so that peace and joy can follow? The first step is to take responsibility for your family and everything over which you personally have authority.

43

Your responsibility determines your authority. There are seven spheres of a society with which everyone interacts:

Religion/Church

Business

Government

Media/Arts/Entertainment

Education

Healthcare

Family

You have a role, or possibly several roles to play in each of these areas. It is our Lord's hope that each of us will make decisions about how we act based upon the gospel of the kingdom. Then, as we are faithful with what has been personally entrusted to us, we will be given more, just as the faithful servant was given authority over 10 cities.

We can see this same pattern in King David's life as he progressed from being a shepherd, to being victorious over the lion, the bear, and Goliath, to serving as an armor bearer to King Saul, then to leading men in Saul's army. David eventually advanced to leading his own men from the cave at Adullam. Then he became the King of Judah and finally the King of Israel. David was given a kingly anointing, but he grew into it. Acts 2:29-30 tells us that David was also a prophet. David's personal intimate relationship with God moved him through the priestly, kingly and prophetic anointings setting an example for us and pointing the way to Jesus. Jesus calls us to be kings and priests.

Revelation 5:10 And have made us kings and priests to our God;And we shall reign on the earth."

The Power of a Transformed Mind

The first step in reigning on this earth is to get your heart right. It begins by recognizing that all of your righteousness is as filthy rags. You need a savior and that savior is Jesus. Acts 2:36 says that God made Jesus both Lord and Christ. Lord means supreme ruler. Jesus needs to be the king in your life.

The gospel of the kingdom is not merely a salvation message. Salvation begins with receiving Jesus Christ. He desires to have relationship and intimacy with us that we might know Him. Through the word of God, prayer, the gifts He has given, and fellowship with the brethren, He takes you through a process by which you begin to take dominion over sin in your own life. He wants to teach you to rule, to reign and to establish the good news of the kingdom in your life. He wants you to have this power because the key to transforming a city begins with your transformed mind. I like what Bill Johnson says in the Supernatural Power of a Transformed Mind page 3:

"However, the mind is actually a powerful instrument of the spirit of God. He made it to be the gatekeeper of Kingdom activity on earth. The great tragedy when a mind goes astray is that God's freedom to establish His will on earth is limited. The mind is not to be tossed out; it is to be used for its original purpose. If the mind weren't vitally important to our walk with Christ and our   commission, Paul wouldn't have urged us to 'be transformed by the renewing of our minds.' In fact, only a renewed mind can consistently bring Kingdom reality to earth."

Romans 12:-2 And do not be conformed to this world, but be transformed by the renewing of your mind, that you may prove what is that good and acceptable and perfect will of God.

Ephesians 1:17-21 that the God of our Lord Jesus Christ, the Father of glory, may give to you the spirit of wisdom and revelation in the knowledge of Him, the eyes of your understanding being enlightened; that you may know what is the hope of His calling, what are the riches of the glory of His inheritance in the saints, and what is the exceeding greatness of His power toward us who believe, according to the working of His mighty power which He worked in Christ when He raised Him from the dead and seated Him at His right hand in the heavenly places, far above all principality and power and might and dominion, and every name that is named, not only in this age but also in that which is to come.

2 Peter 1:4 tells us that God has given us great and precious promises that we might be partakers of the divine nature. Our heavenly Father is totally righteous and holy. He will not and cannot violate His word or His commands. Based on the law, we all deserved death due to our sin. Nevertheless, God who is totally righteous and holy, is also love. He demonstrated His love towards us while we were yet sinners. He sent His Son to live and then to die for us that the righteous requirements of the law might be fulfilled through Him. All that is required on our part is to acknowledge our sin and repent. Repent

means to think differently, or to change your mind. Your mind is changed through the written and spoken word of God. As you spend time with Him, your mind will be changed, or transformed, which will lead to righteous acts, Thank you Lord for your great and precious promises that enable us to associate with your divine nature!

Government Transformed

The transformation of a society will come through individuals as they are transformed through their personal relationship with their heavenly Father. I had the privilege of attending a prayer meeting at my state capitol when the House was in session. There I witnessed a perfect example of transformation affecting legislation.

A senator shared with the group her testimony of how she had come to know Jesus Christ and how her personal relationship had grown over 5 years as she walked through a sickness. It was awesome to see how a personal relationship with Jesus through prayer, Bible reading and fellowship in a small group changed her life. The love and intimacy this senator had with our Savior evident. At one point in the testimony, the senator touched her tummy and a tear began to roll down her cheek as she said, "And God began to talk to me about the sanctity of life." And then she blurted out, "And I was pro-choice."

I marveled at what I had witnessed. First, a personal relationship with Jesus did what seemingly no protest could do. Second, this senator became a witness to a very diverse audience. I have no doubt in my mind that the way the senator voted on legislation dealing with the unborn changed the day God spoke to her.

We must never forget that a transformed society will be accomplished one person at a   time. The most effective transformer of society is a person who has a personal daily relationship with Jesus Christ, and who prays and obeys His leading each day.

How to Establish the Kingdom in Your Sphere

There are 7 spheres in society. They are the church (or religion), business, government, media, education, health-care and the family. Applying the gospel of the kingdom in your life and in your family is obvious. But how do you apply it in other spheres? Let me give you a personal example from my career in business.

After seven years in the ministry I went back to work in the corporate world with a software company for a season. I felt like a failure initially because I thought I had abandonned full time ministry. It took a little while for me to realize that, first, I was still a minister of the gospel, and, second, I was still in full time ministry. The only difference was that my check came from a for-profit employer. A minister simply means servant. We are all God's sons and daughters. We serve our Father in the kingdom. I believe we are all called to be ministers in the sphere we currently occupy. In my new sphere, I still prayed for others, shared the gospel, and used my prophetic gift to establish the gospel of the kingdom. The only difference was that I reached an audience who typically did not attend a church on Sunday.

How did I establish the gospel of the kingdom? I did it through a daily personal relationship with Jesus. I daily ran into challenges where I would ask the Lord in prayer what to do. I was the training manager responsible for all internal training and the external training of our customers. Our customers consisted of Fortune 100 companies that included 5 of the top 10 enterprises in the world. Understanding that the kingdom of God is righteousness, peace and joy and that righteousness was the first thing mentioned, I would ask the Lord, "What is the right thing to do? Lord, would you give me wisdom about how to solve this problem?"

Now the truth was, while I was a training professional and I had acquired my MCSE, I felt overwhelmed by the responsibility of training Fortune 100 companies with - new and ever changing technology. However, scripture taught me that I could do all things through Jesus Christ who strengthens me. So I had confidence in my Lord. I also knew that biblical principles work regardless of whether they are implemented by a Christian or not.

I have already mentioned that God taught me that the major principles of war are biblically based. I had applied these principles in the military, so I now applied them in the corporate world. The application of these biblical principles helped me to turn around an unprofitable training department. Later another department within my company asked for help. Then one of our vice presidents asked me to help him with another division.. Next I was asked to develop the frame work, processes and procedures for a department that was still in the idea stage. Within 6 months that department successfully processed over one half billion dollars. I also trained leaders from our customers' companies, and helped them develop strategies and solutions for their problems.

I became my company's *change management expert* with little formal training. The wisdom found in God's principles was sufficient for me. What is change management? Transformation!

The best example occurred when GM contracted our company to deploy a solution to 40,000 people in 5 countries. The first deployment took 13 months. That was too long, and the deployment was considered unsuccessful. In the second deployment, I was invited to help train GM's leaders and provide a deployment strategy to go along with our improved technology. This time our service was deployed to 40,000 people in 5 countries in 4 months. Two of GM's leaders whom I trained received promotions.

All these things were accomplished by combining my limited knowledge with the biblical principles God taught me in the military, and then seeking Him personally for wisdom in each situation. I applied the same principles I had used in local churches to a business environment. After three years of growing success, various VPs, the COO, and the CFO began coming to my office. They would shut the door and say something to this effect, "OK, Tim, we like how you are solving these challenges for us, but we do not understand how you are doing it. How are you doing this?" At this point, I would share with them about my personal relationship with Jesus Christ, and about how God had given me a gift of wisdom.

I believed the scripture that said I could do all things through Christ who strengthens me. Hence, I expected God to help me when I asked for wisdom. My company and our customers benefited from the application of biblical principles. When I was called upon to consult with our customers, the company set a value of $200.00 to $250.00 per hour for my services. Most often, all the advice I offered was firmly based upon the biblical principles I teach.

Bill Johnson in <u>The Supernatural Power of a Transformed Mind</u> page 51 says it best:

"A renewed mind destroys the works of the devil so that earthly reality matches heavenly reality. It proves the will of God not just in word but in deed. It heals the sick, frees those enslaved to sin, brings joy where there was sadness, strength where there was weakness, explosive creativity, and world changing ideas and inventions where there was lack of invention. It causes the Kingdom of God to be expressed "on earth as it is in heaven." That's normal Christian living."

What keys have we learned about David's pattern?

- King David demonstrated how important regular fellowship with God is in establishing the kingdom, because it brings about a renewed mind.

- Only a renewed mind can bring kingdom reality to earth.

- Jesus Christ fulfilled the righteous requirements of the law so that we might have fellowship with God and renew our minds.

- God wants each person to establish the kingdom in their own life first. As they are faithful, God will give them more responsibility and authority.

- The transformation of society begins with the transformation of a mind, one person at a time.

Chapter 5

The Key to Unity

In David's kingdom, there were numerous organizations and systems consisting of diverse people, each with unique skills and responsibilities. There were armies, priests, Levites who sang, government officials, Levites who clanged cymbals, gate keepers, Levites who played instruments, watchmen, judges, business people, prophets, shepherds, teachers, etc. The list of functions, systems and organizations is huge. When David began to bring back the Ark of the Covenant to set it in Zion, he drew 30,000 choice men together from all of these areas. He gathered them into a unified team.

In the last chapter we focused on the importance of the individual in the kingdom of God. But a kingdom is made up of many people and organizations, each one performing different functions. This chapter focuses on the need for teamwork. For a team to work well, people must be connected together, working in harmony like a body. A kingdom must be united in order to stand.

1 Corinthians 12:20-22 But now indeed there are many members, yet one body. And the eye cannot say to the hand, "I have no need of you"; nor again the head to the feet, "I have no need of you." No, much rather, those members of the body which seem to be weaker are necessary.

One of the most urgent calls I hear in the body of Christ today is a call for unity. Unity is essential to establishing the gospel of the kingdom. However, over the last 20 years, I have come to believe that unity for unity's sake leads to comprise.

As I have attended pastors' prayer meetings I have heard them talk of meeting together to pray so they can get to know each other. They cannot work together unless they have relationship. There is often an implication that some greater action will result in the future which will change their city or region. They have the greatest of intentions. But, unless some of those in attendance are actually spiritual catalysts, then they simply continue to do what God made pastors to do – care for, feed and nurture their people. Psalm 23 said it best: the good shepherd makes the sheep lie down. God made pastors to care for people.

Relationships among leaders are very important to maintaining unity. The real question is, "What initiates the uniting of the body of Christ on a *major* scale?" This major work occurs through spiritual catalysts whom God has gifted and deployed in cities and regions around the world. King David was the catalyst that God used to establish the kingdom in the Old Testament. Even at a young age his catalytic attitude was revealed when he encountered Goliath. In 1 Samuel 17:9 he declared, "Is there not a cause?" Spiritual catalysts are warriors with a cause.

As I have said, God, who is a man of war and the commander of the hosts of heaven, taught me a lot through my experience in the military. In my career, I had the opportunity to work with the Army, Navy, Air Force, Marines and Coast Guard. I can tell you that they each have their own culture and ways of doing things. These differences can often lead to communication challenges. However, certain values were instilled in each group during boot camp. Thisenabled these uncommon groups to work together as a team. These were the principles and values that enabled us in Desert Storm to build a coalition force consisting of many different nations These same principles will work in the church, which also has varied cultures and the resulting communication challenges.

The key to unity in the church is a biblical principle referred to in the military as the principle of objective. This is a common mission, a common cause or a common purpose that brings unity. As I have received orders, traveled half way around the world, and worked with total strangers from various militaries to accomplish a common mission, I have learned that:

- I build relationship faster and get to know others better by working together on a common objective.
- The overall mission brings diverse people and organizations together, while each unique mission is woven together to support the overall objective.

Think about King David and his experience with establishing the kingdom. A common purpose drew all the leaders together at Hebron. That purpose was to make one king. Bringing back the presence of God to Mount Zion was the   common objective that drew

30,000 together under King David. These were major corporate events in the long term campaign to expand the kingdom. The expansion of the kingdom, the establishment of the tabernacle, and fighting common enemies is what kept them unified.

I believe that the key to unifying the body of Christ in a community long term is setting an objective to "transform their community through the presentation of the gospel of the kingdom of our Lord Jesus Christ." With this overall long-term objective in mind, leaders with strategic wisdom will be able to weave strategic corporate events together in support of the long-term objective, just as David did. This will lead to teamwork and cooperation among the body of Christ that has rarely been seen.

It is my conviction that there are people in each church, city and county whom God has pre-positioned to help connect the body of Christ. They are spiritual catalysts who will unite the body around a common cause. They come from all walks of life and represent the different spheres of society. But one thing is certain: they love Jesus with all their hearts. God has gifted these spiritual catalysts with wisdom and a strategic mindset to ensure that the gospel of King Jesus is represented in power and fullness. I pray that the Lord will help us recognize and honor these gifts.

The Power of Unity

In 2003 the Lord sent Brenda and me on an assignment to Nassau, Bahamas to prophetically declare that it was time for the body of Christ to connect. Little did we know that this was a gateway city to the Americas. We learned through the author of America a Destiny Unveiled, Tellis Bethel, that one of the purposes of the Church in the

United States is to set an example of how to unite in spiritual battle. In his book he referenced the exact same thing God had used in 1991 to give me the pattern for CONECT: (page 62-63)

> The historical unification of fifty individual states to form one nation is therefore representative of God's desire for individual believers to function as one body with Christ as the head. It should be noted that America has always played a leading role in uniting the military forces of her allies. Her bringing together of allied nations was crucial in driving Iraq's invading army out of Kuwait during the 1991 Gulf War. This "power of unity" created solidarity on the home front that culminated in the release of power on the battlefield. As a result the "enemy" was expelled and the lives of the "oppressed" were restored."

As I have stated before, God used the military to teach me about biblical principles of war. In my book <u>Biblical Principles and Strategies: the Art of Corporate Spiritual Warfare</u> I teach on the principle of mass. On page 67 it says, "Mass is one of the most important principles in warfare because it defines combat power…" What does the bible teach?

Leviticus 26:8 Five of you shall chase a hundred, and a hundred of you shall put ten thousand to flight; your enemies shall fall by the sword before you.

Matthew 18:19 Again I say to you that if two of you agree on earth concerning anything that they ask, it will be done for them by My Father in heaven.

These scriptures are perfect examples of the power of mass. Remember this defines combat power; and armies exist to project power to enforce the will of the government they represent. Understanding this principle will help you see and create strategic opportunities.

For example, in the United States we have a "National Day of Prayer" on the first Thursday of each May. One scripture that I hear preachers quote frequently is Deuteronomy 32:30. It says that one puts a thousand to flight and two ten thousand. Because I understand the principle of mass, I see opportunity. I think, "Wow! If one puts a thousand to flight and two ten thousand, then what if a million people pray? What if I can add one more to that number? How much more exponential power would be developed if we had a million and one, what about a million and two?" While it is hard to accurately count exactly how many do pray on any given day, I do know that the most effective day will probably be the day on which the most people pray. Hence, anything I can do to add another person exponentially increases the impact I can personally make on the power of prayer projected in my nation.

I also know that the perfect time to turn my attention to my community is while everyone is gathered to pray for my nation.. With that amount of prayer power being projected, I know that our adversary's spiritual forces are being greatly stretched. This is the perfect time to take advantage of his limited forces to make local advances.

Local churches representing every stream and denomination in the body of Christ pray   specifically on the National Day of Prayer. What draws local churches together to cooperate and pray? Is it unity? No! It is a common objective. That objective is to pray for our nation concerning specific prayer targets during a specific time frame. This is the same principle applied by King David when he drew together 30,000 to bring back the presence of God to Mount Zion.

What -have we learned about the pattern?

- A common purpose, or common objective, is what leads to unity.
- Unity is essential in order to apply the principle of mass and increase the power projected through prayer. Every person is essential.

- If a leader understands the biblical principles of objective and mass then they will be equipped to see and create strategic opportunities to advance the kingdom of God in their region. .

Chapter 6

Prophetic Words with Signs and Wonders

In the last several chapters, I have been laying a foundation in order to put the story of Operation Rolling Thunder in context. To broaden the context, we need to look at the roles that prophetic words, and signs and wonders have played in Operation Rolling Thunder

The Role of the Prophetic

People with a prophetic gift are forerunners. God uses them to declare His purpose and intent. In both the Old and New Testaments, we see God sending His servants the prophets to warn people, comfort them and prepare them for what was to come. In 1 Corinthians 12 and Romans 12 we see that prophecy is a gift that functions today, and that God intends it to bless us.

Romans 12:6 Having then gifts differing according to the grace that is given to us, let us use them: if prophecy, let us prophesy in proportion to our faith...

Amos 3:7-8 Surely the Lord God does nothing , Unless He reveals His secret to His servants the prophets . 8 A lion has roared! Who will not fear? The Lord God has spoken! Who can but prophesy?

Isaiah 48:3 I have declared the former things from the beginning; They went forth from My mouth, and I caused them to hear it. Suddenly I did them, and they came to pass.

However, if the word God gives is not received in faith then people will not be blessed. I think Barbara Wentroble in her book Prophetic Intercession, page 128, says it best:

Judah and the inhabitants of Jerusalem were told, first of all, to believe the word of the prophets and they would prosper. The prophetic word is given to God's people for their success. The word, however, will not benefit if it is not embraced in faith.

2 Chronicles 20:20 "...Believe in the Lord your God, and you shall be established; believe His prophets, and you shall prosper."

Let me give you an example. On December 14-15, 2003, Dutch Sheets and Chuck Pierce ministered at Sonrise Chapel in Everett, Washington during their 50-state tour. Dutch and Chuck are modern day expressions of the gifts of apostle and prophet. They delivered a prophetic message to our state during two meetings. There were a few key things that really made an impression upon me as they spoke prophetically. These quotes come from a transcript of the message they delivered.

> Chuck Pierce – "I am going to connect you with those from the past that you need to be connected to... I am going to properly connect some of you to giftings and anointings...So there is going to be a connection of old and new."

> Dutch Sheets – "In this hour you are bringing all of the body of Christ into fullness and we are reconnecting... We are reconnecting with destinies and the giftings and the callings even of the ancient peoples, Lord, the native peoples. There is coming a new soaring on the reservations of Washington...This is an eagle state! Revelation, strength, vision, warring mantle, warrior mantle... Washington shall be connected..."

The gift of the prophet declares what is to come, while the gift of apostle prepares to build what the prophet prophesies. In Dutch and Chuck's message for Washington State they spoke of connect, connecting or reconnecting over 21 times. CONECT was something I had worked on for over 10 years at that point. The issue becomes how to apply what the prophet declares.

There were more prophetic words regarding connecting given throughout the year, but these are good examples of what I had heard by the time I was asked to oversee the National Day of Prayer for Washington State in December of 2004. Combining that event with the new Global Day of Prayer was the first opportunity I saw with regard to the prophetic word about connecting. Here was an opportunity to connect an old prayer event to an older prayer event. God had prepared me for this season; I knew it was my time. I would help the body of Christ in Washington connect as the prophets had declared.

1 Thessalonians 5:20-22 says, "Do not despise prophecies. Test all things; hold fast what is good." In the late 90s, I had opportunity to implement CONECT in local churches. From 2002 to 2004 I tested it in other countries to determine if it was cross cultural. I had not yet had an opportunity to test its ability to unite churches in cities, cities in counties, and counties in a state. The premise is that biblical principles work regardless of the size of the application. Now, God had given me a state to test and prove CONECT.

The Role of Signs and Wonders

Forerunners face great challenges. Depending upon your gift, you may see things so far off that no one understands you right now. Hence, God may have to encourage you with signs and wonders. Think about Moses when God sent him to lead the children of Israel out of bondage. He was God's answer, the one that God sent to deliver them, and in Exodus 6:9 it says:

> *So Moses spoke thus to the children of Israel; but they did not heed Moses, because of anguish of spirit and cruel bondage.*

God then instructed Moses to go speak to Pharaoh. Moses replied something like, "Yeah right. Your people won't listen; and this heathen ruler surely won't listen to me either." So, in Exodus 7:3, God says that He is actually going to harden Pharaoh's heart so that He can multiply signs and wonders. That way Pharaoh and the children of Israel will know that He is God. There were a number of signs, from Aaron's rod turning into a snake to the various plagues, but I want to highlight the seventh plague that served as a sign. God sent hail, thunder, lightning and rain as judgment on the enemy and as a sign to His covenant people. I love what Hebrews says:

> *Hebrews 2:2-4 how shall we escape if we neglect so great a salvation, which at the first began to be spoken by the Lord, and was confirmed to us by those who heard Him, God also bearing witness both with signs and wonders, with various miracles, and gifts of the Holy Spirit, according to His own will?*

According to the Strong's Concordance the word sign in verse 4 here is semeion. It is translated in the King James Version as sign, wonder, miracle or token. This word is used 61 times in the New Testament and, in every case except one, it refers to an event that people would refer to as supernatural. But in 2 Thessalonians 3:17 we see this word used in a different way. Let's take a look at a few translations:

> *2 Thessalonians 3:17 The salutation of Paul with my own hand, which is a sign in every epistle; so I write. KJV*

> *2 Thessalonians 3:17 I, Paul, write this greeting in my own hand, which is the distinguishing mark in all my letters. This is how I write. NIV*

2 Thessalonians 3:17 Here Is My Greeting In My Own
Handwriting—Paul. I Do This In All My Letters To Prove They Are
From Me.   Holy Bible, New Living Translation ®, copyright © 1996,
2004 by Tyndale Charitable Trust.

In the scriptures above, the word "sign" is used by Paul to indicate that this letter belongs to him. It is proof that he wrote it. I believe that God uses signs and wonders as proof of His ownership, too. Whenever His people do what He has directed them to do, they make church His-story (history). Sometimes God will perform a sign or a wonder just to put His mark on it - to say, "This is mine. My people did this at My leading therefore I am going to put My signature on this page of history so everyone will know it's Me."

Think about the ultimate forerunner, Jesus. When He began his ministry, only His mom and John the Baptist recognized Him at first. So His heavenly Father gave Him a little supernatural encouragement by speaking to Him from heaven, telling Him that He loved Him and He was well pleased. In John 2, Jesus performed his first sign at a wedding where He turned the water into wine. Because of this sign His disciples believed in Him.

When Jesus left this earth, He sent the apostles to preach the gospel of the kingdom. It says in Mark 16:20 that the Lord worked with them confirming the word with signs following.

So God can use signs and wonders to deliver His people, encourage them, help them believe, and confirm His word spoken by prophets.

Let's take a look at a few things that God used as signs in the Bible.

- Genesis 9:17 – a rainbow

- Genesis 17:11 – circumcision

- Exodus – 10 plagues

    a. The 7th sign was thunder, hail, lightening and rain

- Numbers 17:10 – Aaron's rod that budded

- 1 Kings 13:3-5 – word given by prophet confirmed by split altar

- 2 Kings 20:8 – shadow moved backwards on sundial

- Isaiah 7:11-14 - prophetic word of virgin bearing a child as a sign

- Isaiah 8:3 & 18 – prophet used name of his son as a sign and a prophetic symbol

- Isaiah 20:2-3 – Isaiah walks naked for 3 years

- Ezekiel 12:6-13 – the prophet and his acts were a sign to Israel

- Ezekiel 20:12 – the Sabbath

- Matthew 6:14 – Jesus' three days in the tomb

- Mathew 24 – wars, rumors of wars, false Christs, famines, pestilences, earthquakes, false prophets, and the gospel of the kingdom preached in every nation

- Luke 21:25 – sun, moon, stars, sea, waves

- John 4:48-54 – Jesus heals a boy of a fever

- John 6:12-14 – Jesus multiplies bread

- John 10 – blind eyes opened

- 1 Corinthians 14:22 – tongues

- Revelation 12:1-3 – sign in heaven

We have already seen in Mark 16:20 that God confirmed His word delivered through His apostles with signs following. We also saw that God does the same for His prophets. It is part of their job description.

Hosea 12:10 I have also spoken by the prophets, And have multiplied visions; I have given symbols through the witness of the prophets.

The nature and timing of the assignments of forerunners makes their jobs really challenging. So, if what God has given them to prepare or deliver is far off, then He may give them some personal encouragement along the way. I experienced that when He sent Brenda and me to Nassau, Bahamas in 2003.

Here is the story. Upon my return from Desert Storm I entered the ministry. I began to teach the biblical principles He taught me and I developed CONECT. I used the principles of CONECT as we mobilized local churches in the city of Springfield Oregon during the March for Jesus in 1994. I also used them in various corporate prayer events; and I implemented them in a few churches in the late 90's. At times, we saw some very dramatic results.

In 1999, I returned to the corporate world until 2002. It turned out to be a marvelous time as I applied the principles of CONECT to the corporate setting with a great amount of success. At the end of 2002, I returned to the ministry and I felt the Lord leading me to test some of the concepts in CONECT on a larger scale. Within a short time, in early 2003, the   president of a business college,

Pastor Johnson, in Nassau, Bahamas contacted me and asked me to come to Nassau to teach their leaders. At first, I said no.

Later I told the Lord, "If you want me to go, then you have to provide the financial provision and I am not going to ask anyone." Within two weeks, someone in California sent us a check for $2,000.00. I told Brenda, "Well, I guess we are going to Nassau." This was to be the very first time I delivered CONECT in the context of a city with a view to connecting with government and business with the intent of transforming society.

God Confirms His Word with Signs Following

Daniel 4:2-3 I thought it good to declare the signs and wonders that the Most High God has worked for me.

We spent a week in Nassau and delivered the message of CONECT to church leaders, business leaders and government officials. In our last meeting, we met with our hosts and their church. When the time came to pray for the sick, God moved miraculously. The most dramatic sign occurred when Brenda prayed for the pastor's wife. Her leg was swollen terribly. No sooner did Brenda lay hands upon her than her leg began to return to normal size. The change was so dramatic and so quick that the congregation began to scream as it changed before their eyes.

To bless us the next day the congregation sent us to an island where the rich and famous go for holidays. It had pink beaches and beautiful turquoise waters. I loved it, as I grew up in Florida. We had the most incredible day on this   island. The weather was perfect, the food was the best, and we ended our day on the beach with a folding chair under an umbrella overlooking the water. The water was flat calm. I looked at Brenda and said, "You know, there is only one thing that would make this day perfect, and that is if I had some waves and I could body surf."

So we went in the water. Over the course of an hour the waves picked up and I rode four great waves all the way into shore. I was satisfied and thought, "Wow, this is a pretty interesting coincidence." Then we got out of the water, and do you know what happened? The water went flat. The waves quit as soon as we got out. We were walking down the beach and I was saying, "Pinch me! This did not really just happen, did it? If this is so, then God did this just to personally bless me and encourage me."

Right when we were having this conversation, a Bahamian came running down the beach, breathing heavily, and said, "God sent you here, and you are coming back."

God used the signs of healings and the waves to let us know that we had delivered His word and had completed His assignment. These were wonders that really encouraged us.

Isaiah 44:24-26 I am the Lord, who makes all things, Who stretches out the heavens all alone, Who spreads abroad the earth by Myself; Who frustrates the signs of the babblers, And drives diviners mad; Who turns wise men backward, And makes their knowledge foolishness; Who confirms the word of His servant, And performs the counsel of His messengers; Who says to Jerusalem, 'You shall be inhabited,' To the cities of Judah, 'You shall be built,' And I will raise up her waste places...

Psalm 86:17 Show me a sign for good, That those who hate me may see it and be ashamed, Because You, Lord, have helped me and comforted me.

What have we learned about the pattern?

- Scripturally, God used signs and wonders to confirm the word of apostles and prophets.
- God has given prophecy as a gift, and it works today.
- God uses prophets today to declare what He is going to do.
- God uses signs and wonders to help His people believe, to claim a work as His own, and to confirm His word spoken by prophets.

Operation Rolling Thunder Kit

Get equipped to mobilize your church and city. There are 4 audio CDs, a DVD and Power Points that accompany the vision and explain how to form a Transformation Task Force on a data CD, an agenda, Public Service Announcements for the radio, brochures, and much more. www.ORTPrayer.org

Chapter 7

Values and Kingdom Culture

Operation Rolling Thunder is a strategy that applies the pattern we learned by studying King David. The first thing we learned was how important it is to connect leaders. The second thing we learned was the importance of having a common objective and establishing 24/7 prayer, praise and worship in a city.

We not only want to look at the pattern of what David did, but also at how he did it. What values did the culture in his kingdom express? These values are important to maintaining unity in the body of Christ.

Love

King David is the author of Psalm 18:1. He begins it with, "I will love You, O Lord, my strength." This is the Psalm from which Operation Rolling Thunder was derived. King David established a tabernacle for the Ark of the Covenant, so the presence of God could dwell on Mount Zion. He did this because he loved God and His presence. Love is the foundational value in the kingdom.

Love for our Lord Jesus, love for His Church, and love for mankind must be the motivation   behind all that we do in presenting the gospel of the kingdom. 1 Corinthians 13 teaches us that it does not matter how gifted you are; if your gift works without love, it is worth nothing. Galatians 5 teaches us that faith works through love. Jesus taught us that there is no greater love than to lay one's life down for one's friends.

The only place you can get this kind of pure love is from God. We need to be rooted and grounded in His love. That comes from spending time daily in His word and in prayer. Knowledge of the Bible without prayer will lead to legalism. Prayer or being led by the Spirit, without the word of God can lead to lawlessness. If we love God, we will spend time with Him. As we spend time in His presence we will be transformed. We will be changed from glory to glory and prepared to "re-present" Jesus as both Lord and Savior.

Honor

In the American culture, honor took a huge hit in the 1970s. This filtered over into the church, and we still suffer from its influence today. Honor is one of the kingdom values that I strongly believe God wants to restore in the body of Christ. Have you ever noticed that there are more leaders and people honored by name in David's kingdom than in any other in scripture? Honor is a key value expressed in kingdom culture. 1 Peter 2:17 sums it up well:

"Honor all people. Love the brotherhood. Fear God. Honor the king.

Honor means to value, prize or esteem. Respect is closely associated with honor. It can be given through the use of titles, such as referring to a judge as "your   Honor," referring to the policeman as "Officer," to your minister as "Pastor, or to a man or woman by adding Mr., Mrs., or Miss depending upon marital status and age, ."

In the military, honor is one of those absolutely essential values that make the system work. Honor is rendered in order to respect levels of authority and responsibility. It not only flows up the chain of command but it goes down, too. Honor is expressed to all through name, rank and common military courtesies such as salutes. Remember, God is called Lord of the Hosts (armies) more than any of the other Jehovah names.

Now, do some people abuse honor? Yes they do. They may abuse titles. Some people dishonor others by overstepping their bounds of authority. Jesus identified some Pharisees in Luke 11 who had these problems. Because some people abuse the truth, does that mean the truth should not be applied? I don't think so.

Another way honor can be rendered is by receiving the gifts and contributions people make. For example, as I have traveled across Washington to mobilize the body of Christ, I find the gifts of God (1 Corinthians 12, Romans 12, and Ephesians 4) represented in each city and most local churches regardless of the denomination. I have come to the conclusion that most of what is needed to transform each community is already there.

In the last three years, we have seen God move incredibly through Operation Rolling Thunder. But I have realized from the start that whatever has been accomplished was only due to those faithful intercessors and unknown prophets, who for decades have prayed God's heart over my state. Generations both young and old have contributed. I think of Coach Roach in Federal Way who is 78 years old. God used him to connect the body of Christ and mobilize prayer in his city for decades. I also think of Bridget, who was 18 years old. God used her to mobilize a stadium prayer event in Spokane. As I've traveled across my state, I have looked for opportunities to honor those unsung heroes.

An attitude of honor creates an atmosphere that releases the gifts to operate. For example, people with a prophetic gift often come to me and tell me how that gift began to stir in them. This is because I value and welcome the gift of a prophet and the gift of prophecy. Prophets are an important element in developing effective strategies to transform our cities.

But there is so much more than just gifts that function in the traditional church setting. Every person has gifts, talents, abilities and value. The key to transforming society is not the building we call a church, but it is the people. God gave apostles, prophets, evangelists, pastors and teachers to equip the church to do the work of the ministry. Truly, people are our greatest resource because contained in them are the multifaceted gifts of God. Getting to know God's people is like a treasure hunt to me. It is exciting to discover the gift in each person.

Love motivates leaders to search for these gifts and then to utilize each person's gift to contribute to the overall mission, while fulfilling their personal destiny.

God is so passionate about honoring the gifts He has given us! I'll share in Chapter 10 how God used an 80 mph windstorm and a very large offering to get my attention regarding this matter. He drove home the point that I was to honor the apostles and prophets and the emerging city networks in 2007.   If we honor them, we will receive the benefit of the gift God gave them.

The Benefit of Honor

I learned a principle many years ago from Pastor Larry Henderson. He taught us that "familiarity breeds contempt." In other words, sometimes you know someone so well, that you do not see the gift that God gave them. You know their past; you know their failures; you knew them "when." By not recognizing their gift, you devalue it.

Jesus faced a similar problem. His family did not recognize him, either. In Mark 6:4 it says:

> *But Jesus said to them, "A prophet is not without honor except in his own country, among his own relatives, and in his own house."*

Jesus also taught us in Matthew 10:41 that if you receive a prophet in the name of a prophet you will get a prophet's reward. If you receive, a righteous man in the name of a righteous man, you will get a righteous man's reward. Everyone I know has a combination of gifts. Some gifts are more prominent than others are.

Jesus, who embodied the fullness of God with every gift, was only able to heal a few sick people in his hometown of Nazareth because of unbelief. They knew Him before he was baptized by John. In Mark 6:7 we see Jesus calling the 12 unto Himself and sending them to cast out demons. The 12 received the benefit of the anointing, or gifting, in His life because they respected and honored the gift God gave.

In my case I have three strong gifts according to certain assessments. They relate to the Ephesians 4 gifts of apostle, prophet and teacher, with a strong administrative gift as well. There are some close to me who only see aspects of the gifts God has given me. In 2005 I remember a specific example One minister only saw my administrative gift therefore that congregation saw no miracles. Another minister saw and honored the apostolic gift in my life. I know this because they acknowledged it when they called and asked me to pray for their team before they went on a prayer assignment in their city. This occurred shortly after Operation Rolling Thunder had ended. God gave a sign. For three days we saw three to five thunderstorms a day roll across cities in our state. Even the weatherman on Channel 7 news reported about the "rare thunderstorms, rolling across Washington." The team that I had been asked to pray for included a prophet who knew nothing of the scriptural basis for Operation Rolling Thunder. During the prayer assignment, this prophet prophesied out of Psalm 18:6-14 which is the scripture that ORT is based upon. The leader noted that within an hour or two of the finish of their prayer assignment, a thunderstorm occurred. This really encouraged them, as s/he remembered what God had done for me through Operation Rolling Thunder. I believe the reason that they saw this sign was that they recognized the gift and therefore benefited from it.

Some things are taught, while other things are caught. The anointing is something that is caught more than taught. . The anointing comes through association and honor. God confirmed the ministry's respect for the authority and gift by giving them the same scripture and the same supernatural sign that God had given me through ORT. They benefited from the authority that God had given

78

me. This is a perfect example of 2 Corinthians 10:15 where the sphere of influence and authority was enlarged through the exercise of their faith. This happens through respectful relationships.

Humility

Proud leaders will not unite the body of Christ, but the humble will. David was a humble man. Humility goes hand in hand with honor. One of the biggest challenges I've seen in mobilizing the body of Christ is false humility. I'd like to share with you what the Lord taught me one day regarding humility.

Who does the bible say was the most humble man on the face of the earth? Moses! Numbers 12:3 tells us so. Who was the author of the book of Numbers? Hebrew tradition says it was Moses! Now can you imagine someone saying that they were the most humble man on earth? Most of us today would think that statement sounded proud.

Let's compare Moses to Saul. In 1 Samuel 10, when Saul was chosen as king, they could not find him because he hid himself. They had to inquire of God to discover that he had hidden himself behind some equipment. In 1 Samuel 9 Saul reveals his heart by saying that his tribe is the smallest and his family is the least. Doesn't that sound humble?

Moses was given the assignment to lead the children of Israel out of bondage. Reluctantly, he said, "Yes Lord." Humility agrees with God and allows God to place us where it pleases Him. In Moses' case, it was leading a nation. Moses was the gift through which deliverance came to God's people. Hence, Moses was humble.

Saul on the other hand was not humble. It did not matter what God said. Saul thought his   opinion, ideas and judgment were more right than God's. For example, in 1 Samuel 9 the prophet Samuel anoints Saul king and then he tells him the signs God will give him to confirm the word. The signs occur just as the prophet said. But in chapter 10, when God gets ready to reveal Saul as king, Saul hides himself. He did not agree with what God said of him. This is a form of false humility. This is actually pride because Saul had exalted his opinion over God's decision.

Here is another example of humility. In Matthew 18 the disciples were discussing with Jesus would be greatest in the kingdom of heaven. In verse 2 Jesus called a little child and placed the little child in the middle of His disciples. The word for "called" the little child is the same word used when Jesus called His 12 disciples. It is the same word used in Acts 13:2 where the Holy Spirit separates Barnabas and Saul for the work He called them to. Then Jesus said:

> *Matthew 18:3-4 "Assuredly, I say to you, unless you are converted and become as little children, you will by no means enter the kingdom of heaven. Therefore whoever humbles himself as this little child is the greatest in the kingdom of heaven. Whoever receives one little child like this in My name receives Me.*

The Holy Spirit asked me a question. Who became the center of attention? I said the little child did. Then it hit me. Humility is being willing to be placed where God wants you. If He needs you to be at the center of attention or at the head, then humility says, "Yes Lord."

The little child was humble in that he allowed Jesus to place him at the center of attention because it suited our Lord's purpose.

This is a very important principle in the kingdom. Humility is to agree with God, with what God says about you and what He wants to do through you.

We should not err, as some have, by promoting themselves through pride. False humility is wrong, too. Both actions are sinful. They miss the mark. The key to exercising humility is love. 1 Corinthians 13 teaches us that love is not proud. Humility also says, "I am incomplete on my own. I need others and their gifts in order to fulfill my destiny in Christ." I honestly believe the gifts that are needed by the body of Christ to transform a city are available right there in that city, if, through love and humility, we honor one another. Love, honor and humility are necessary to unite the body of Christ. We need each other.

What keys values are essential in kingdom culture?

- Love
- Honor
- Humility

Chapter 8

Spiritual Catalysts

On May 25, 2006, I was invited to the National Day of Prayer
(NDP) headquarters in Colorado Springs, CO to consult with their
national area leaders regarding a prayer strategy for 2007. Two other
ministers, who specialize in the area of transformation, were also
invited. One of those ministers was well known in the transformation
movement and had produced a number of books and documentaries
on the subject. The NDP leadership shared that they were interested in
being involved in establishing 24/7 prayer in cities and being involved
in city transformation. After the leadership had received this well
known minister's input they asked for mine.

The input I shared was differed from his because the gifting in
me is different. I appreciate other ministries that document and analyze
testimonies from various places experiencing transformation. Their
work has been a tremendous blessing to the body of Christ and they
excel at research and analyzing results. My function is not that of an

analyst; I am a catalyst. According to the The American Heritage® Dictionary catalyst has the following definitions:

1. In chemistry, it is a substance, usually used in small amounts relative to the reactants, that modifies and increases the rate of a reaction without being consumed in the process.

2. One that precipitates a process or event, especially without being involved in or changed by the consequences.

A catalyst is something or someone who precipitates a process or an event and can increase the rate of reaction. God has given gifts to the body of Christ that are, by nature, catalysts. These catalysts are the gifts of apostle and prophet.

I am a catalyst – a leader with vision and strategy who inspires people to action; and I lead by example. I activate people by teaching and empowering them to apply what they have learned to a specific purpose. We had just mobilized the greatest volume of 24/7 prayer in my state's history. We had also formed the first Transformation Task Force made up of leaders from the 7 spheres of society. I had not recorded this history. I had equipped people to make history. With this understanding in mind, I offered my input to the council.

The Catalyst's Effect on Prayer in a State

It is not my intention to get into a theological debate about the modern day gifts of apostle and prophet, but I do want to talk about *the functions* of the apostolic and prophetic gifts. If we understand their functions, we will be better equipped to identify the catalysts God has already placed in each geographic region. If you want to study this more, I recommend books by C. Peter Wagner, John P. Kelly or John Eckhardt.

First, the prophetic words delivered through Dutch Sheets and Chuck Pierce in 2003 helped me connect two events through Operation Rolling Thunder. Second, God deposited in me an apostolic gift to fulfill the mission He assigned to me.

To accomplish my mission He has given me an anointing to unite and mobilize the body of Christ as an army, with the goal to establish 24/7 prayer in the pattern of the restoration of David's

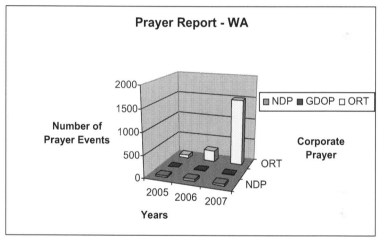

tabernacle. This mission supports presenting the gospel of the kingdom to transform cities with power. Operation Rolling Thunder is the resulting catalytic strategy that empowers people to transform their communities.

Remember the definition of catalyst. It is a small substance that when added to a reactant increases the rate of reaction. ORT is the catalytic strategy that increased the effectiveness of National Day of Prayer and Global Day of Prayer in Washington State.

After I took responsibility for National Day of Prayer (NDP) and the Global Day of Prayer (GDOP) in Washington State in 2005, prayer increased dramatically. The Global Day of Prayer grew from 2 events to 9.. GDOP was the newer event and, though few in numbers, we had more than most states. In fact, Washington State, one of the least churched states in America, was one of the top states in the US for GDOP events in 2006 and 2007. NDP grew from 37 events to about 50. NDP has been around since the late 80's and the number of events did not change significantly compared to its history in my state.

Connecting these two events with Operation Rolling Thunder is a strategy that empowers small churches to unite in raising a canopy of prayer over their community 24/7/365 days a year, while gathering leaders from all 7 spheres of society to strategize for presenting the gospel of the kingdom. ORT grew from 80+ days of 24/7 prayer (in 2005?) to over 1,512 days in 2007.

This graph illustrates the effect of a catalyst on prayer in Washington State. (*See chapter 13 for more current results.*) By 2007 the state of Washington, in particular Whatcom County, was covered by 24/7 prayer 365 days a year.

Here are some practical outcomes of this strategy.

- Our CONECTer in Whatcom County, Pastor Jason Hubbard, heads up prayer at Christ the King in Bellingham. This church alone grew by 1,000 people within two years.

- Another pastor from Whatcom County reported that, in 2005, their county was statistically considered the least churched county in the US. By 2007 they came off the bottom of that list.

- A small business, Merit Emergency, also covenanted with us in 2006 and they saw a 100% increase in gross revenue.

Now, am I saying that the catalyst is responsible for all of these results? No! A catalyst won't work unless other elements are there to form the reaction. Christ the King has many programs and does an excellent job reaching out to the community. The owner and contractors of Merit Emergency work very hard. However, both leaders attributed a great portion of their increase to ORT. They recognized the gift in my life and choose to use the strategies I provided. Ephesians 4:16 says that when each part of the body *does its share*, it causes the body to edify itself in love. We need each person and organization to do their parts.

Catalysts, Authority and Strategy

The reason I am sharing candidly about my life is that it is one illustration of the benefits that can be realized by recognizing a catalyst. A catalyst is anointed by God with strategy and authority. If you recognize a person who is a catalyst, and use their anointing, then you have positioned yourself to be blessed by them. They can bless your church, your business, and your community. I believe that God has placed catalysts in every community and in sphere of society. They are keys God has given to help transform your community. *I pray that you will catch a vision to mobilize the body of Christ in your community through Operation Rolling Thunder and discover the treasure -of catalysts God has placed in your region.*

The Function of Apostles

Now back to apostles. What did apostles do in the book of Acts? They laid the foundation of the church. They pioneered new works, blazed trails to new places, and, when problems were raised in the church, they sought God for wisdom. They had authority given by God, and, as they delivered His word, sometimes signs and wonders followed their ministry.

We understand from 1 Corinthians 3 that the apostle Paul was a wise master builder. A master builder understands plans and structures very well. Like Moses and King David, they may not be the ones to actually build the structure, but they are the ones God entrusts with His plans. They are like spiritual architects, who provided the plans. Others do the actual building, while the master builder oversees.

Those with an apostolic gift have an eye for the big picture. They are catalysts who break ground and initiate the building process. They also have divine authority from the Lord to fulfill their assignments. God will, at times, confirm His word to them with signs following. They are leaders.

My military experience taught me that in peace time officers with strong managerial skills do well at keeping things operating smoothly. They rise to the forefront because in peace smooth operations are esteemed. However, when war comes, senior leaders seek aggressive officers to take command. I've heard of one unit going through 4 commanders before they found the one who was the right leader. Leaders have the kinds of gifts that win battles. Both managerial and leadership gifts are always needed because both functions are always necessary. It is more often in wartime that the officers gifted as managers need to follow and support officers gifted as leaders.

In Ephesians 4:11, Jesus gave us apostles, prophets, evangelists, pastors and teachers to help mature the church until we come to the unity of the faith. In our culture almost every minister is referred to as pastor whether they are a true pastor or not. The true pastoral gift is expressed in Psalm 23. A pastor makes the sheep lie down and feeds them in a place of peace and rest. That is the way God made pastors. They work best with a flock because God made that gift to be relational. The good shepherd knows every sheep by name. Due to that need for intimacy, we need many pastors.

However, can you imagine the pressure that people put on the pastoral gift when they expect their pastor to do everything? It is very frustrating to try to use a tool for a function for which it was not designed. Now that city transformation has come to the forefront, people in churches often want their pastors to take the lead in changing their cities. This can be an unrealistic expectation if that pastor is not also a catalyst.

Transforming a city requires strategy. God has called those with the apostolic and prophetic anointings to mobilize an army and to develop prayer and action strategies appropriate for their assigned areas. Many pastors have not been given those divine strategic tools. Neither have they been taught the basics of how to develop strategy. As people put unrealistic expectations on pastors, they become frustrated they put in a position to fail. Is it any wonder that the people who hold these unrealistic expectations become frustrated as well?

Each gift imparts a portion of God's heart. The evangelist imparts God's heart for the lost; the pastor imparts God's heart for the family; the teacher imparts a love for God's word; the prophet imparts a love for the presence of God and the His spoken word. In Paul's epistle to the Corinthian church, we discover the function of the gift of apostle. God made apostles to lead the body of Christ in spiritual war and to develop strategy.

2 Corinthians 10:3-4 For though we walk in the flesh, we do not war according to the flesh. For the weapons of our warfare are not carnal but mighty in God for pulling down strongholds...

The word translated as "war" in the Greek Strong's Concordance means to serve in a military campaign or to execute the apostolate. Apostolate means the office of an apostle. A study of the etymology of the word for apostle shows that it was first a Greek/Phoenician seafaring term used to refer to a leader of a convoy. Then it was used for the commander of a military expedition. Finally, it was used to refer to the ambassador general sent to represent a government. Later the word was used by Jesus. Because apostle was not a religious term, but a military term, I think the Lord, being a man of war, used this word to emphasize the function of this gift.

The word translated "warfare" in the Greek means warfare or apostolic career. It is where we get the word strategy and it means generalship. Hence, apostolic people will have a mind for spiritual war. They also are gifted with wisdom and strategy to know how to project power in order to present the gospel of the kingdom in love. Strategies may include prayer, acts of kindness, utilization of resources, etc., Due to the nature of the gift, apostles tend to be strong leaders. They take the initiative to launch campaigns to employ the strategies God gives them. They take action. Apostles are also given to prayer and the word of God. Through this regular communion with God, He gives them revelation.

These gifts still operate today. I believe God has deployed apostolic gifts in every sphere of society. These people have an eye for God's specific strategy for their assigned area. Much of their communication comes directly from God along with words from prophets. In Apostles and Prophets the Foundation of the Church by C. Peter Wagner on page 37, he says:

> "God can and does, reveal His plans directly to apostles. But He also reveals His plans to prophets who, in turn, communicate them to the apostles."

The Function of Prophets

Prophets are vital spiritual catalysts as well. We see so many wonderful examples in both the Old and the New Testaments. Jonah's prophesying led to a whole city repenting. He was a catalyst. John the Baptist was a catalyst and prepared the way for Jesus. In the book of Acts we see the prophets Judas and Silas working alongside Paul and other apostles. But I think Jeremiah describes the function best:

Jeremiah 1:9 Then the Lord put forth His hand and touched my mouth, and the Lord said to me: "Behold, I have put My words in your mouth. See, I have this day set you over the nations and over the kingdoms, To root out and to pull down, To destroy and to throw down, To build and to plant."

This scripture illustrates what the prophet is equipped to do: to create to war, to pull down and destroy, and to build and plant.

Prophets work hand in hand with apostles. Prophets have extra sensitive ears to hear and spiritual eyes to see what God is communicating. The prophets often declare what God is going to do. As Amos 3:7 says, God does nothing unless He tells His prophets. They are an important key to gathering what I like to call spiritual intelligence.

How Prophets and Apostles Function Together

The apostles are gifted with the wisdom to know how to initiate action in order to see the prophetic word fulfilled. Ephesians and 1 Corinthians teach us that apostles and prophets are key to the foundation and that they are to go first when establishing God's purpose in the earth. First does not mean the highest, as in hierarchy. *It means first in order of application, as in the first steps.* These two gifts are like the point of the spear. They engage the enemy first. They are governmental gifts. These are spiritual catalysts that initiate and lead with strategy. God made them to tear down strongholds and then to lay foundation for others to build upon. If we follow the order God gave, we will all be blessed as the catalysts will greatly increase the effectiveness of the rest of the reactants.

Ephesians 2:20 having been built on the foundation of the apostles and prophets, Jesus Christ Himself being the chief cornerstone...

1 Corinthians 12:28 And God has appointed these in the church: first apostles, second prophets, third teachers, after that miracles, then gifts of healings, helps, administrations, varieties of tongues.

The apostle has a kingly anointing. 2 Samuel 11:1 tells us that there is a season when kings go to war. They go to war to establish a kingdom. We have entered a season of spiritual war now upon the earth. It appears as if God is restoring gifts to the body in the reverse order they were lost after Jesus returned to heaven. The first gift lost was that of the apostle and the last major gift being restored is that of the apostle. Hence, we are entering into a season of strategic spiritual war as the gift of apostle is restored.

I learned in my time at the Navy War College that armies exist in order to enforce the political will of their governments. Today, God is mobilizing the Church to extend the government of Jesus.

Isaiah 9:7 Of the increase of His government and peace there will be no end, Upon the throne of David and over His kingdom, To order it and establish it with judgment and justice from that time forward, even forever. The zeal of the Lord of hosts will perform this.

Another pattern that I observe is that King David had two people with prophetic gifts who worked side by side with him. Gad was a seer and Nathan was a prophet. I can tell you that in my travels around Washington I have met many people who have these prophetic gifts functioning in their lives. Many of them exist in places where their gift is not understood and therefore are not received. Whenever they get around me, their gifts begin to function. Often they will ask me why that occurred. It occurs because I receive their gifts and welcome their function. I understand that we need everyone's gift to function in order to mature.

Ephesians 4:16 from whom the whole body, joined and knit together by what every joint supplies, according to the effective working by which every part does its share, causes growth of the body for the edifying of itself in love.

I want to encourage you to look for and receive the marvelous gifts God has given to you in your community. I've focused on apostles and prophets because they are the first and second in function. This in no way minimizes any other gift nor the importance of all the other gifts such as teacher, pastor, evangelist, administrator, gifts of healing, hospitality, giving, deacons, elders, etc. We need ALL the gifts functioning.

The 7 Spheres of Society

Whenever you go to war, it takes a huge team. The Army handles the ground, the Navy the sea, the Marines handle amphibious operations, and the Air Force is primarily responsible for air operations. The Church is likened unto a spiritual army and, just as the US military has different militaries made for to serve different functions, so does the Church.

Several years ago the Lord, by revelation, began teaching me about what I call the 7 spheres of society. It consists of the church, business, government, media, education, healthcare and the family. It does not matter if we talk about the Americas, Africa, Europe or the Middle East. In any society there are people working in and passionate about each of these areas. The transformation of a society will not occur within the four walls of a church building. It occurs when the church gets out of their buildings and back into their communities. That's when society can be changed.

After the Lord had begun to speak to me regarding the spheres of society, I learned that I was certainly not the first to receive this revelation. God had spoken to Loren Cunningham, who founded YWAM, and to Bill Bright, who founded Campus Crusade for Christ, decades earlier about the 7 mind molders of nations. Their list is slightly different than the 7 spheres but this is a good example of two wonderful apostolic (strategic) gifts God gave the Church. It is also an example that when God does something He never just speaks to one, but He speaks to many.

Each sphere of society in every city is different. I believe God has called people in His Church to affect every sphere. I also believe He has pre-positioned people throughout the world to discover and present God's unique prayer and action strategy to effect transformation in each region.

If we look at any specific geographic area, the 7 spheres are represented there, and the spheres overlap. For example, the sphere of government can enact laws that affect businesses, families, churches, healthcare, and the media. Media – which consists of arts, entertainment, news, magazines,   TV, radio, newspapers etc. –

touches people through information and business through advertising. We could weave an elaborate thread through all these spheres of society very easily, as they are all very complex systems.

I believe the Church's role is to affect transformation. Therefore the church needs to approach transformation like King David did when he expanded his kingdom. He did it through war. Spiritual war begins by assembling leaders and applying biblical principles of war. (See appendix A).

I learned in the military that, while major strategies and principles never change, the combination of those principles is constantly changing. These principles are important because they are practiced in the kingdom realm in heaven, and God desires us as individuals to practice them in His kingdom on earth.

The first principle to apply in war is the principle of objective, one of the most timeless principles of war. It has been taught for over 2,500 years because it works. It works because it is biblically based. The principle teaches us that the objective must be clearly defined.

The second step is to destroy enemy forces. To move to step two, intelligence must be gathered in order to develop an effective strategy. It is important to identify your enemy's capabilities, intentions and dispositions, while also identifying your allies and their capabilities. Until the intelligence gathering step is completed, you are ill equipped to develop the best strategy. Once a strategy is developed the enemy should be engaged and defeated. The last step is to occupy the territory. (See Appendix A for training resources and Appendix B for CONECT, which empowers leaders to apply these principles in their areas.)

Forming a Transformation Task Force

In the transformation of David's kingdom, the first step was to draw together the leaders in a city for the nation (1 Chronicles 11). ORT follows David's pattern using a Transformation Task Force (TTF) as a means to identify and draw together strategic leaders. A Transformation Task Force consists of 7 councils formed with Christians who work in and are passionate about their specific spheres of society. You will recall that we are looking for catalysts. Catalysts are people who have an apostolic or prophetic view and who will initiate action. Here are some examples of where you might find some of your leaders.

- Church – Fivefold leaders, church staff, elders, deacons, intercessors, prayer leaders, etc.

- Business – Owners, employees, investors, etc.

- Government – elected officials, bureaucrats, appointed officials, clerks, civil servants, police departments, fire departments, etc.

- Education – Principals teachers administrators, support staff, and parents in public schools or private schools, colleges, universities, etc.

- Healthcare – Doctors, nurses, specialists, care givers, administrators, people in the insurance industry, etc.

- Media – Writers, dancers, journalists, actors, radio/TV personalities, producers, publishers, artists, etc.

- Family – Everyone passionate about family, as well as the special ministries and government agencies with a focus on serving people.

Leaders do not have to be apostles or prophets. Look for people who are passionate about seeing Christ presented in their sphere as well as having the insight and authority that are important for developing an effective prayer and action strategy. Good candidates will have a heart to unite the body of Christ. Some may be very passionate about prayer and intercession, while others may be strategic thinkers. While God may lead you to recognize new people of potential, some may already very obviously be leaders recognized for the apostolic or prophetic gift they carry.

Don't worry about titles, or about who might be called apostle or prophet. *What we are looking for is the function.* 1 Thessalonians 5:21 provides an excellent principle to walk by. It says to "prove all things and hold fast to that which is good." Another good principle is to know those who labor among you. Watch for a kingdom mindset along with the expression of the kingdom values of love, honor and humility.

Pastor Jake Dragseth shared this thought, "Apostles are chosen by God and recognized by peers. They are not 'self appointed.' Why? Apostles are given insight, revelation, and levels of authority which cannot be assumed. Simply put, apostles are given information and passion not given to others. Many people are pursuing the title for prestige and validation when God has not anointed them."

Another important thing to watch for is fruit. Trust me, the apostles and prophets in your midst will have their character proven and their gifts tested over time. Their fruit will become evident. All we need to do is to love and honor each other in humility. When fruit is evident, I strongly advise that it is   beneficial to all to recognize and honor the gift. If you receive a prophet in the name of a prophet, you will get a prophet's reward. It works the same for the apostle or any other gift.

The Purpose of the Transformation Task Force

The definition of a Transformation Task Force (TTF) reveals its purpose.

Transform – to change in condition, nature, or character; to convert.

Task – a definite piece of work assigned to, falling to, or expected of a person; a duty

Force – strength; energy; power; persuasive power; power to convince; mental or moral strength; might, as of a ruler or realm; strength for war.

The TTF is a force of people who have united with a duty to transform their society. They are responsible to pray that God's kingdom come and His will be done on earth as it is in heaven. In addition, they have a mandate to present the gospel of the kingdom to their assigned territory. This task force should exist until their assigned territory is either completely transformed or until Jesus comes back.

Why do we need to draw together the leaders representing all 7 spheres of society within a specific geographic area? Because each sphere affects other spheres we need wisdom:

Proverbs 21:22 A wise man scales the city of the mighty, And brings down the trusted stronghold.

Proverbs 24:6 For by wise counsel you will wage your own war, And in a multitude of counselors there is safety.

There is wisdom and safety in a multitude of counselors. A TTF provides a place to draw together catalysts and to glean God's specific strategy for your region.

How to Start a Transformation Task Force

A Transformation Task Force can be formed within a church, a city, a county, a state or a nation. The key is to draw together people, from the different spheres, who are passionate about a common geographic area. The best way to start a TTF is to rally around a common cause bigger than any one individual or group in support of an event like Operation Rolling Thunder.

Each year I have hosted a Kick Off event which has drawn together leaders, intercessors, watchmen and others passionate about prayer and transformation. In addition to presenting the vision, tools and training, we have breakout sessions hosted by chair people representing each of the 7 spheres of society. The breakout sessions have served to gather those who are passionate about their spheres and then to identify what transformation would look like in their sphere. This has helped me to devise a prayer strategy for our state to be launched during Operation Rolling Thunder. Operation Rolling Thunder ties national and global prayer events together in order to support God's purpose nationally and internationally. It enables the church to "pray globally and connect locally" with the long-term view to present the gospel of the kingdom through prayer and action.

Events such as National   Day of Prayer have leaders and

people who play key roles. NDP encourages the formation of a steering committee. They recruit church, city, county, and state coordinators for their events to be launched on the first Thursday in May each year. They have done a powerful job, and there will always be a need for people to fill these roles. So what is the difference between a steering committee and a Transformation Task Force?

While a steering committee and a coordinator exist for an event, the TTF exists for the long term. In addition a CONECTer serves as the contact point for the TTF, as well as others. You will find more details about how to start a TTF, and training for CONECTers, watchmen, intercessors, and leaders in the appendix.

24/7 City Prayer and Mobilization Training Package

Our CONECTers have discovered the best way to mobilize cities quickly. This training and mobilization package includes a case of books, brochures, and an Operation Rolling Thunder Kit with CDs, DVDs and Power Points - everything a leader needs to launch the strategy in their city.

Get yours today from www.ORTPrayer.org or
www.KingdomLeague.org.

Chapter 9

Operation Rolling Thunder – 2005

Now that I've declared to you the revelation God gave me, I'll explain the history of the vision and the results of applying it.. By following the ancient pattern I saw in David's kingdom, we have seen signs and wonders just as in the Old Testament.

Some leaders have suggested that I do not share about the supernatural signs and wonders God has given around ORT. They thought that some would reject ORT because of this. I, however, have chosen to follow another pattern I see in scripture, which is that each year during Passover God had the children of Israel remember the signs and wonders by which He delivered them from Egypt. Therefore, I've chosen to remember all God has done the best I can in order to accurately report what has happened.

The Bible teaches us that Jesus is the same yesterday, today and forever. God does not change. We should not be surprised when God uses signs today like He did then. Signs are a way for God to put His mark, or signature, on a page of "His-story." We should not be enamored with the signs, but neither should we ignore them. Even we use signs to give direction, provide   warnings, mark the location of services, advertise a product, etc.. Why should we be surprised if God chooses to put His signature on a page of history? Think about it this way. It is God's "sign-nature." His nature is supernatural and His character never changes. He is the same yesterday, today and forever, is He not?

In this testimony, many leaders and people will be mentioned, but all glory and honor go to our Lord Jesus Christ, the King of Kings and Lord of Hosts.

The Genesis of Operation Rolling Thunder

In December, 2004 I was asked by Kathie Cassady to take responsibility in representing National Day of Prayer for the state of Washington in 2005 On December 14, 2004 I met with Kathie Cassady (National Day of Prayer - Area Leader West States), Dr. Flo Ellers (Glory Global Ministries) and Father John Roddam (St. Luke's Episcopal Church, Ballard, WA.). I had just learned about Prayer Week, based out of the United Kingdom, and the Global Day of Prayer that was birthed in Africa. Due to the prophetic words I had heard, I knew this was an assignment I was to take as I had been uniquely prepared for it.

So here is the scenario. National Day of Prayer fell on May 5, 2005, the Global Day of Prayer fell on May 15, 2005 and Prayer Week fell right in the middle. The Global Day of Prayer included a strategy calling for 10 days of 24/7 prayer followed by 90 days of outreach. I doubted that the leaders of these major prayer events had collaborated together. I assumed that each group had merely prayed and obeyed the leading of our Lord.

As the four of us began to pray the Lord led me to Psalm 18:6-14. This scripture basically says that when *the Psalmist cried out, God heard him and His voice thundered from heaven in response to scatter his foe.* Then it became so very obvious to me that Holy Spirit had just orchestrated this tremendous crescendo of prayer around the world. Because I understood the principle of mass and the pattern in scripture with regards to the restoration of David's tabernacle, I knew this was a strategic opportunity.

It was in this context that I strongly sensed a direction in my spirit: 10 days of 24/7 prayer! Every day we pray, God answers; as each day rolls over, we continue to pray and God continues to answer. Hence God wanted us to launch "Operation Rolling Thunder." It is about the voice of the Lord.

Psalm 18:6-14 In my distress I called upon the Lord, And cried out to my God; He heard my voice from His temple, And my cry came before Him, even to His ears. Then the earth shook and trembled; The foundations of the hills also quaked and were shaken, Because He was angry. Smoke went up from His nostrils, And devouring fire from His mouth; Coals were kindled by it. He bowed the heavens also, and came down with darkness under His feet. And He rode upon a cherub, and flew; He flew upon the wings of the wind. He made darkness His secret place; His canopy around Him was dark waters, And thick clouds of the skies. From the brightness before Him, His thick clouds passed with hailstones and coals of fire. **The Lord thundered from heaven, And the Most High uttered His voice,** *Hailstones and coals of* *fire. He sent out His arrows and scattered the foe, Lightings in abundance, and He vanquished them.*

Operation Rolling Thunder – The Name Confirmed

I shared this scripture with John, Flo and Kathie in our prayer meeting. Then Dr. Flo Ellers, minister to the First Nations people (remembered the prophetic word that Dutch gave in chapter 6 told us that God had told her to host a "Mighty Warriors Conference" on the Tulalip Reservation on May 11-15. Guess what the name of the primary speaker was? His name was "Lott Thunder." Flo did not know about the Global Day of Prayer strategy. She had merely prayed and obeyed the leading of the Lord. We all marveled with laughter at this first sign and wonder. (Isaiah 8:3, 18 and 20:3)

Hence, I accepted the assignment to head up the National Day of Prayer for Washington State, while simultaneously taking responsibility for Operation Rolling Thunder (ORT). I also promoted the Global Day of Prayer in my state. I saw this as a divine assignment, including the restoration of David's tabernacle, the 24/7 prayer movement as well as the uniting of the body of Christ through local churches who were passionate about long-term transformation.

David instituted 24/7 prayer, praise and worship and God blessed him with success in expanding the kingdom. Every reformation mentioned in scripture followed David's pattern. Every king who reinstituted 24/7 prayer, praise and worship saw a degree of blessing because that created a place for the presence of God. When those kings stopped 24/7 prayer they lost the blessing.

Any church, city, county,   state or nation that chooses to follow the pattern King David set can see the same blessings He saw. Operation Rolling Thunder is a strategy that equips people to apply the pattern that King David used. I hope ORT helps you create a place where our Father's presence is welcome.

Establishing 24/7 Prayer in a City or Region in One Day

There are many churches in the body of Christ who are passionate about seeing 24/7 prayer offered up 365 days a year. Unfortunately, most local churches do not have enough people to maintain a continual prayer watch. However, if we break down the responsibility church by church, we can establish 24/7 prayer to cover our region today.

In 2005 there were 10 days between the National Day of Prayer and the Global Day of Prayer. The message we presented to prayer coordinators and church leaders was: *the goal is to cover 10 days with 24/7 prayer. Can you find 10 churches in your city each one willing to commit to covering that day with 24/7 prayer?* In 2005 we found churches in 10 cities in Washington who worked together to cover their city with 24/7 prayer while simultaneously praying with the national and global prayer initiatives.

10 Cities in 2005 – Seattle, Tukwila, Olympia, Federal Way, Sammamish, Kirkland, Coupeville/Oak Harbor, Monroe, Bellingham and Deer Park.

The churches in each city selected different ways to actually do 24/7 prayer. Olympia followed the International House of Prayer model and had one church serve as the host for the whole city. Federal Way had one church cover each day and host a corporate prayer gathering for the city. Hence, each day the location of corporate prayer changed. Tukwila used a phone prayer chain for their ten days. The examples of how 24/7 prayer was established as each community prayed and obeyed the leading of the Lord. But the one *common theme* was *uncommon cooperation*. As each church did their share, a canopy of prayer was lifted over their city. The prayer agendas for the National Day of Prayer, Prayer Week and the Global Day of Prayer greatly benefited as well. Truly, this kind of cooperation was uncommon in Washington.

Prayer Targeting Strategy

Part of the strategy was to realize that many churches would participate with these national and international prayer events. We understand the power behind the Biblical principle of agreement found in Deuteronomy 32:30 where one puts a thousand to flight and two puts ten thousand. There is exponential power in agreement.

We encouraged local churches to agree with the prayer strategy presented by their state, national and global leaders. But each community has unique challenges that hinder people from receiving the gospel and the church from making disciples. Who would know better how to pray for each community but the church in each community? Hence, while churches are gathered to pray for state, national and international prayer initiatives, that is the perfect time to focus their prayers on the transformation of their local communities.

I provided training to prayer coordinators, intercessors and watchmen on how to gather spiritual intelligence through a course in our Spiritual War College called "Watchman and Intercessor Training for Teamwork and the Corporate Anointing." The intent was to equip the church in cities and counties with the ability to develop their own unique prayer strategies to launch during this time. One of the best examples of how this was applied occurred in Island County.

The NDP Coordinator was Jacque Hildreth. She caught the vision, and, due to research, discovered that their county had the highest number of meth labs in the state as well as the highest number of 8th graders who had tried meth. Hence, the churches in her area prayed regarding this problem. Four days after they initiated this strategy I heard a report on Channel 7 news. Olympia had just announced the formation of a drug special task force made up of special agents whose sole mission was to focus on the meth problem in the state of Washington.

God Confirms His Word and Strategy

Some of our prophetic people began to ask me questions because they understood the power of mass concentrated prayer. One question I heard a number of times was, "Tim, do you expect earthquakes as a sign?" To which my response was, "No, if God is going to give a sign, I believe it will be thunderstorms."

Rainbow Appears During Tukwila GDOP Event Picture provided by CONECTer Jenny McCoy

On May 5th, the National Day of Prayer, 80 plus churches in 10 cities launched the 10 days of 24/7 prayer. On May 13th, my wife, Brenda, directed me to the weather channel where thunderstorms were forecast in Washington.

May 15th was the Global Day of Prayer. We had two events in our state. The first was a stadium event in the city of Tukwila. Global Day of Prayer coordinator, Jenny McCoy, reported that, during their prayer for the nations, a rainbow appeared over their stadium. What are the odds that a covenantal sign God gave in Genesis 9:13 would show up during their prayer for the nations? Needless to say they were very encouraged and excited by this tangible sign.

The second event was hosted by Dr. Flo Ellers and Pastor Merle Williams at the "Mighty Warriors Conference" on the Tulalip Reservation with Rev. Lott Thunder. I had the privilege of being invited to join with the First Nations' leaders in praying with the Global Day of Prayer strategy on the Global Day of Prayer.

Level 9 Geomagnetic Storm Recorded at 11:50 GMT on 5/15/2005

The next day a local business man, Michael Boyle, emailed me and told me to check out an article reported by the National Oceanic and Atmospheric Administration (NOAA). NOAA had issued a space weather warning because they observed an extreme weather event on the sun on Sunday May 15, 2005. Using a K-Index that ranges from 0 to 9 they measured a level 9 geomagnetic storm. http://www.noaanews.noaa.gov/stories2005/s2437.htm .

NOAA also reported that such a geomagnetic storm could cause widespread system voltage control problems and blackouts. Spacecraft and satellites could be impacted as well. Reports from the NOAA Space Environment Center indicated that the US did indeed experience these kinds of problems.

I had expected to God to do something dramatic on the day of the largest prayer gathering in history. But I would have never thought of a storm on the sun. It was a sign and a wonder in heaven.

Acts 2:19 I will show wonders in heaven above and signs in the earth beneath: Blood and fire and vapor of smoke. NKJV

My wife, Brenda, and I had lived in Washington about 10 years and I don't think I had seen more than three or four thunderstorms the whole time. On May 17, 2005 through May 20, 2005 we saw three to five thunderstorms per day go across cities in Washington. Some included hail. On May 20th I heard the weatherman on Channel 7 news report about the "rare thunderstorms rolling across Washington." This was another sign and a wonder. I believe this was from God to encourage His people that He heard them and was responding from heaven.

Psalm 18:13-14 The Lord thundered from heaven, and the Most High uttered His voice, Hailstones and coals of fire. 14 He sent out His arrows and scattered the foe, lightings in abundance, and He vanquished them. NKJV

Luke 21 describes what it will be like in the last days. It speaks of wars, famines, pestilences, earthquakes and signs in the heavens. Verse 36 goes on to say that when we see these things "watch therefore, and pray always." Remember, God uses signs and wonders to encourage His people. God saw common people gather to pray with uncommon cooperation and He responded with signs and wonders to encourage His people to continue to "watch and pray."

A Challenge Is Issued

Churches in 10 cities in Washington PROVED they could cover their city with 24/7 prayer if they just worked together with each local church taking one day. Then a challenge was issued which is one of the primary goals of Operation Rolling Thunder. If churches could cover their city with 24/7 prayer by working together for 10 days, THEN WHY STOP?

Chapter 10

Unite and Ignite – ORT 2006

The last city to join Operation Rolling Thunder in May 2005 was Bellingham. With only 10 days left before Operation Rolling Thunder commenced, Pastor Jason Hubbard began to mobilize his community. Working with the Holy Spirit and with people passionate about uniting in ongoing prayer, they quickly covered their 10 days of 24/7 prayer.

The strategy and Biblical principles used to lay the foundation for Operation Rolling Thunder were based upon a revelation of the restoration of David's tabernacle and biblical principles of war.

In November of 2005, Pastor Jason hosted a conference called "Unite and Ignite" at Christ the King in Bellingham, Washington. He invited me to present CONECT and the strategy for 2006. Operation Rolling Thunder tied unique corporate prayer events together, while CONECT provided the training, tools and processes needed to facilitate and coordinate massed prayer on a long-term basis. Together they empowered the Church to occupy via long-term strategic action to transform their community. This was the first place that the strategy for 2006 was presented.

The Kick Off for Operation Rolling Thunder on January 28, 2006 was held at the Seattle Revival Center, and was hosted by Pastor Gail Homan. Since National Day of Prayer fell on May 4th, and the Global Day of Prayer fell on June 4th, the goal was to cover each county in our state with 24/7 prayer for 31 days. Once again, Prayer Week fell right in the middle of those two dates. The Holy Spirit had again orchestrated this wonderful crescendo of prayer around the world. So the strategy that year was to find 31 churches in each county or city who would agree to cover at least one day with 24/7 prayer. The message our CONECTers and coordinators presented to their communities was: 31 churches, 31 days. Do you think we can find 31 churches, each willing to take at least one day to cover with 24/7 prayer? We challenged the churches to host corporate prayer events on the National Day of Prayer and the Global Day of Prayer as well. All we asked was that leaders pray and obey the leading of our Lord.

Finally, we challenged the church at large, "If we can do it for a whole month, then why stop?" We asked each local church to prayerfully consider doing 24/7 prayer every month thereafter on the same day as they did during Operation Rolling Thunder.

My role in Washington was to head up prayer and to develop a prayer strategy for my state, as well as to facilitate each community in discovering what their unique prayer strategy would be. With that goal in mind, I formed the first state Transformation Task Force to advise me on a prayer strategy for my state. The premise presented through CONECT is that society is made up of 7 spheres (church, business, government, media, education,   healthcare and the family) and that

God has His people positioned all through society. For example, who would know more about transformation in government than a kingdom minded Christian who served as a senator? I asked leaders from each sphere of society to sit as a chairperson of a breakout session to glean feedback from their audiences. I asked them to answer the following question: "What would transformation look like in your sphere?" My chair people hosted the breakout sessions, and a CONECTer was assigned to record their information. The first Transformation Task Force consisted of:

- Government – Representative Kirk Pearson – 39th District
- Media – Bill Montgomery from KGNW Radio
- Education – Debra Rae – Author ABC's of Culturalism
- Business – Daren Lenard former CEO
- Healthcare – Dr. Karen Johnson
- Church – Pastor Dan Hammer – Sonrise Chapel
- Family – Pastor Gail Homan – Seattle Revival Center

From their input we gleaned a prayer strategy for our state covering each sphere. We also encouraged counties and cities to form the same kind of Transformation Task Forces.

Circum-horizon arc recorded over Spokane WA, June 3, 2006

The result for 2006 was 235+ days of 24/7 prayer mobilized from 12 different counties in Washington during that month. On

June 3, 2006, the last open air event in our state was held in Spokane, led by 18-year-old Bridget Hillier-Vogel. The event was called "Unify." Thirty minutes before their event a very strange weather phenomena occurred over the skies of Spokane. It was called a circum-horizon arc. I received emails from Rev. Dan Grether, who was a witness, along with an article and a picture from the Spokesman Review. A couple of days later, I received an email from Jennifer Kannapel referencing an article published by The Daily Mail titled "A Rainbow of Fire Observed in the Northwest" (June 11, 2006). In the article the phenomena was described as a blanket of fire. Then I remembered the "Unite and Ignite Conference" in Bellingham where the strategy for our state had been proclaimed months before.

On June 3rd we had just seen the most concentrated massed 24/7 prayer in Washington state history for a whole month, the result of uncommon cooperation among churches in 12 counties. The body of Christ had UNITED and now the sky over Spokane IGNITED.

The County of Spokane was mobilized by small business owner, minister and National Day of Prayer Coordinator Shirley Offill. Pastor Tim White, of Tri-County Christian Center, also played a major role in mobilizing churches, not only in his city but also in Stevens and Pend Oreille counties. Pastor Tim shared with me that they saw a great increase in thunderstorms around 24/7 prayer. A report from the Washington State Climatologist regarding the "The Washington 2006 Top Ten Weather & Climate Events" confirms this observation. (http://www.climate.washington.edu/events/2006top10.html) The number 4th ranked event in Washington that year was thunderstorms that hit eastern Washington with Spokane having its 6th wettest month in 126 years. Most of that rainfall occurred in the first 14 days of June with some reports of hail as big at 1' in diameter. This was another place were flooding and mudslides occurred in Washington.

I see this as a visible demonstration and an encouragement from our heavenly Father that He was pleased with the response of local churches all over Washington.

> *Luke 21:25-28 And there will be signs in the sun, in the moon, and in the stars; and on the earth distress of nations, with perplexity, the sea and the waves roaring;26 men's hearts failing them from fear and the expectation of those things which are coming on the earth, for the powers of the heavens will be shaken. 27 Then they will see the Son of Man coming in a cloud with power and great glory. 28 Now when these things begin to happen, look up and lift up your heads, because your redemption draws near." NKJV*

The scripture previously mentioned in Luke 21 says in verse 36 that when we see these things we ought to continue to "watch and pray."

It is not my intent to be enamored with signs and wonders. But at the same time I do not want to neglect the word of God. These are signs of the times and it should encourage God's people. He does hear our prayers, therefore we ought to continue to "watch and pray."

Testimonies from 2006

Whatcom County - Pastor Jason Hubbard reported that 34 churches in 8 cities participated. Whatcom County was the first county in Washington to reach the goal of 31 days of 24/7 prayer. A local pastor reported that Whatcom County was the least churched county in the US. However, this county saw such an increase in salvations that they are no longer the least churched county. Pastor Jason reported that their local church, Christ the King in Bellingham, grew by about 500 that year.

Churches in 12 Counties mobilized 235+ days of 24/7 prayer for Operation Rolling Thunder.

- Whatcom, Skagit, Snohomish, Island, King, Pierce, Thurston, Yakima, Clark, Stevens, Pend Oreille, and Spokane.

Jenny McCoy reported that the churches in the city of Tukwila mobilized their resources and created a virtual fair to reach out to their community for the 90 days following the Global Day of Prayer. Here is a list of some of their outreaches:

- Volunteer Chore Services
- Community Service Projects
- Domestic Abuse Women's Network
- A Hospitality House
- City of Tukwila Parks, Recreation and Human Services
- Adopt a Cop

Testimonies

Business – Bill Merritt of Merit Emergency reported a 100% increase in gross revenue. He   attributed that growth to partnering with our ministry to offer strategic prayer in support of business operations. His wife Gwynn operates Mt. Olympus Hair. She led prayer for a woman who was healed of cancer.

Government – The mayor of Kent told of a growing gang problem and requested help from local pastors to discover a solution that would bless the community.

Healthcare – Those attending a breakout session in the city of Auburn hosted by Apostle Steve Anderson of Answer the Call discovered a unique evangelism opportunity in the area of healthcare. Two nurses reported that their hospital had a reading program for patients but they did not have enough volunteers. Imagine this as a new evangelism strategy! Can you come and read? While you are there, perhaps God will give you the opportunity to pray for someone who is sick.

God's Signature

Chuck Peirce of Glory of Zion Ministries is a prominent minister, prophet and apostle in the US today. Here is a quote from him.

Prophecy: JERUSALEM FLOODS ON 40 YEAR ANNIVERSARY--THE CITY IS TARGETED FOR A HOLY SPIRIT INVASION! Chuck Pierce: May 19, 2007 Glory of Zion Ministries. http://www.lightthehighway.org/en/index.php/Jerusalem_Floods_-_Chuck_Pierce_-_05.19.07

> "During our Feast of Tabernacles Gathering on October 14-15, 2006, the Lord spoke to us and said, "Plant your feet! Ready yourself for change! You are entering a year of shaking and quaking! This year   will be known as the Year of Holy

Spirit! This will be the year the RIVERS will rise! Watch where the heavens open and floods (physical) reach the earth, and document those places! Those are places targeted for a Holy Spirit invasion. Rising flood waters will cause you to move to higher ground. As the River of Holy Spirit rises, you will find yourself moving to the high places. I will position My people on the high places this year. As you worship, I will cause ruling thrones of iniquity to topple. Like Dagon, their head will fall before My Presence! Get ready! I shake loose wicked structures. Watch in the night, and watch Me manifest in the light!"

The National Weather Service reported on December 21, 2006 that Washington State experienced the "November to Remember" as record rainfall fell over a great portion of the state. Seattle had the most rainfall since they began keeping records with 15.63 inches measured at Seatac Airport. Twelve rivers also reached all time record high flood crest levels.

What is interesting is to compare the prophecy with the number of rivers that flooded and the number of counties that participated in ORT. It was the same - 12. The real eye opener was that King County broke every known rainfall record in history. It was also the county that had double the 24/7 prayer in the state due to the work of Pastor Gloria Locken who mobilized cities in west King County, and Deanna Brenner who mobilized cities in east King County. Record rainfall was another sign that God was using to confirm to His people that He was acting powerfully.

Psalm 68:8-9 The earth   shook; The heavens also dropped rain at

the presence of God; Sinai itself was moved at the presence of God, the
God of Israel. 9 You, O God, sent a plentiful rain, Whereby You
confirmed Your inheritance…

Hebrews 2:4 God also bearing witness both with signs and wonders, with
various miracles, and gifts of the Holy Spirit, according to His own will?

The Greek word translated signs in Hebrews 2:4 is used 61 times in the New Testament. It is translated signs or miracles many times, but in 2 Thessalonians 3:17 the apostle Paul uses this word to indicate that this is how he signs his letter. It is his mark.

The prophet Chuck Pierce prophesied about the flooding of rivers. The heavy rain in began only two weeks after the prophet spoke. I believe God was pleased with the response of His people and gave this sign to encourage us to continue. While there are some prophetic words in scripture that will be fulfilled regardless of what people do, most prophetic words are conditional. I believe the reason we saw 12 rivers flood in Washington is because 12 counties participated in Operation Rolling Thunder. To make it even more clear, the county that had twice the volume of 24/7 prayer in ORT broke every known rainfall record in November. Was it a coincidence or a sign and a wonder? You need to decide for yourself. There is no doubt in my mind that God used a sign of rain to put His signature on this page of history. He wants His people to continue to "watch and pray" 24/7 365 days a year.

The Thunderstorm and Financial Miracle

On December 14, 2006, I presented the strategy for Operation Rolling Thunder 2007 publicly for the first time at the Northwest New Wine Network in Everett. The Lord impressed upon me that it was time to speak clearly about the role of the Transformation Task Force and what God expected to emerge out of each city. The Bible says in Ephesians 2:20 that the church is founded on the foundation of apostles and prophets with Jesus Christ being the chief cornerstone.

One of the primary goals of Operation Rolling Thunder is to facilitate the emergence and the gathering together of the apostles and prophets whom God has already placed in communities all over my state. Hence my role as the Washington State CONECTer that year was to simultaneously honor the emerging apostolic networks, and to facilitate their connection with prophets as well as with leaders from the 7 spheres of society. In fact, the Transformation Task Force is actually the beginning of an apostolic council. Every region should have its own Transformation Task Force consisting of kingdom minded leaders from the 7 spheres.

After presenting my message I drove home in an 80 mile per hour windstorm with thunder, lightning etc. As I was driving home, I was talking to the Lord. I said, "Well Lord, is this a coincidence or is this another sign?" I got my answer when I got home. First, trees had fallen all around our neighborhood and I understand that over 1 million people lost power in our area, but our lights stayed on. We also received certified mail that day. In that mail was the largest offering we had received in the history of our ministry. In fact, it was five times larger than the largest offering we had received since 1992.

The major thunderstorm   and the financial miracle occurring on the same day as I presented the strategy for Operation Rolling Thunder spoke volumes to me. It was clear that I had a mandate to carry this message and facilitate the emergence of apostolic networks throughout my state.

Psalm 86:17 Show me a sign for good, That those who hate me may see it and be ashamed, Because You, Lord, have helped me and comforted me. NKJV

According to the Washington State climatologist who reported on "The Washington 2006 Top Ten Weather & Climate Events," the number one event was the windstorm in December and the number two event was the record rainfall in November.

Jeremiah 5:24 They do not say in their heart, "Let us now fear the Lord our God, Who gives rain, both the former and the latter, in its season. He reserves for us the appointed weeks of the harvest.

Joel 2:23 Be glad then, you children of Zion, And rejoice in the Lord your God; For He has given you the former rain faithfully, And He will cause the rain to come down for you — The former rain , And the latter rain in the first month.

Isaiah 44:3 For I will pour water on him who is thirsty, And floods on the dry ground; I will pour My Spirit on your descendants, And My blessing on your offspring...

Chapter 11

The Spirit of the Moravians

ORT 2007

On January 12-13, 2007, we hosted the Operation Rolling Thunder Kick Off at Sonrise Chapel in Everett Washington. Once again it seemed as if God was giving us a sign, as a very strong snow and ice storm hit our state along with "thunder snow" in at least one location. Wikipedia (http://en.wikipedia.org/wiki/Thundersnow) says that a winter thunderstorm is a particularly rare meteorological phenomenon that occurs in regions of a "strong upward motion within a cold section." When I read that definition, it made me think of the condition of my state and the 24/7 prayer movement.

My state is one of the two least churched states in my country, but, there has been a steady rise in 24/7 prayer across Washington. Hence, the strong upward motion of prayer in a cold hard place had God responding to the earth with thunder to encourage His people. It was like God saying, "I hear your cries and I am responding with signs and a voice like thunder from heaven."

Elijah List e-newsletter – October 22, 2007 – Prophet Kim Clement

"During the early part of 2007, God began to deal with me regarding signs that He was sending to the earth through the disruption of weather patterns. God had spoken to me about the fact that this would work in favor of His people and specifically how weather **manifestations in the USA, would be a sign of the dawning of a great spiritual era.**"

The Strategy for 2007

In 2007, the National Day of Prayer fell on May 3rd, while the Global Day of Prayer fell on May 27th. Once again Prayer Week fell right in the middle, giving us a target of 24 days. Here is a summary of the strategy that God gave for that kick off.

- The real goal was to mobilize extraordinary amounts of 24/7 prayer in support of strategic action to transform the state of Washington in all 7 spheres of society.

- The body of Christ is a spiritual army in a spiritual war and God has deployed apostles and prophets throughout cities and regions to mobilize and connect the army of the Lord (2 Corinthians 10:3-4, Ephesians 2:20, and Ezekiel 37:1-10).

- My role was to:
  o Impart apostolic strategy.
  o Mobilize, connect and honor apostolic leaders, prophetic leaders, networks, streams and denominations throughout cities, counties and states.

- o Establish 24/7 prayer in cities and regions through the application of the biblical principles presented through the Christian Outreach Network Establishing City-wide Teamwork (CONECT.)
- o Combine informed prayer with strategic action to transform communities.

- The history of signs, wonders and the growth of 24/7 prayer in Washington during 2005 and 2006 was reviewed.

- The strategy for the National Day of Prayer events was promoted, encouraging an increase of four times more events.

- The strategy for the Global Day of Prayer was promoted.

- The strategy of Operation Rolling Thunder was presented with a focus on:

  - o Using these events to facilitate on going daily prayer in the spirit of the restoration of David's tabernacle and the Moravians who launched the 100 year prayer gathering.

  - o Covering each of 39 counties in Washington by seeking 24 churches to cover 24 days with 24/7 prayer.

  - o Sending the message: We can establish 24/7 prayer 365 days per year in your city or county if we just cooperate, with each church taking responsibility for one day.

  - o Supporting the 2007 goal to mobilize at least 936 days of 24/7 prayer.

- We were to honor, support and encourage the emergence of city and regional networks throughout our state.

o   To demonstrate this I asked the Northwest New Wine Network, headed by Apostle Dan Hammer, to host the Transformation Task Force for our state.

- Chapters of CONECT were presented as a tool to link county and city networks in order to facilitate and coordinate 24/7 prayer with action in support of long-term transformation in cities, counties and the state.

In 2007 the state Transformation Task Force consisted of:

- Church – Apostle Dan Hammer
- Government – Donna Hart & Rep. Kick Pearson
- Business – Bill Merritt of Merit Emergency
- Healthcare – Dr. Karen Johnson – The Johnson Institute
- Media – Stan Lander of GMI Media
- Education – Bob Penny, a retired principal
- Family – unrepresented this year

What the Transformation Task Force Discovered

After the breakout sessions, the chair people presented their findings based upon two questions.

1. What would transformation look like in your sphere of society?
2. How can transformation be measured in that sphere of society?

As each chairperson gave their report, we discovered some unique creative opportunities to partner the church with Christians reaching out in their spheres. We also discovered a common thread that ran through each sphere of society. The people in each sphere wanted a way to connect with other   kingdom minded people passionate about working to transform their spheres of society. Hence the first answers to the two questions were:

1. Transformation begins by connecting like minded people in their specific sphere of society, while simultaneously maintaining connection with the other 6 spheres.

2. The transformation in answer one can be measured by creating meetings at specific times and places for each of the various spheres of society.

I was unaware of what the feedback would be from the breakout sessions of the Transformation Task Force groups, but God had already given the solution to connecting like-minded people among the spheres. A Chapter of CONECT provides a way for emerging city and regional networks to connect the seven spheres of society by city, county and state.

Chapters of CONECT

CONECT (Christian Outreach Network Establishing City-wide Teamwork) is an acronym for a vision built on proven biblical principles. It is a tool given by the Lord. It forms a communication structure that works in local churches, cities, counties, states and nations. It is designed for the time when the body of Christ would begin to connect in order to effect transformation in their areas of society. Some of the biblical principles applied in ORT come from CONECT. A chapter of CONECT provides a way to:

- Gather the elders at the city or county gates.
  - o Honor local apostles, prophets, evangelists, pastors and teachers.

- o Connect leaders from the 7 spheres of society to form a Transformation Task Force.
- Mobilize, connect and coordinate intercessors and watchmen.
- Connect kingdom minded local churches and ministries passionate about reaching the same geography.

Commission a person or team to serve as a CONECTer (net-worker) to connect leaders, churches and ministries within a defined geography such as a, church, city, county or state.

For a detailed explanation of CONECT see Appendix B.

Releasing the Spirit of the Moravians

Pastor Jason Hubbard, who had served as our CONECTer in Whatcom County for 2006, had the unique privilege of visiting Herrnhut Germany. It was there that Count Zinzendorf and the Moravians started a 100-year prayer vigil with 24 men and 24 women praying one hour per day. This launched the modern day missionary movement.

Pastor Jason is one who is passionate about the presence of the Lord. He carries with him a revelation of the beauty of the Lord and message of the cross. I asked him to share about an encounter he had with our Lord in Germany. As he shared, the passion grew and excitement built until he prophetically proclaimed God's intention to release the spirit of prayer and of the Moravians over the Northwest. A wave of the Spirit of God swept the audience. Many ended up on their faces, crying out and weeping as a spirit of grace and supplication was poured out. After a time I handed the microphone to Apostle Dan Hammer who stood as a leader for the Church in the Northwest to prophetically receive the spirit of the Moravians that had been released.

Truly our Father is passionate about seeing a 24/7/365 prayer movement sweep cities around this world in the spirit of the restoration of David's tabernacle.

Thunderstorms Roll across Washington

Operation Rolling Thunder began on May 3rd in 2007. Corporate prayer events for the National Day of Prayer were scheduled all over our state; and Operation Rolling Thunder was tying NDP with the Global Day of Prayer through 24/7 prayer.

One of the roles I filled in 2007 was as the State Coordinator for National Day of Prayer. My responsibility was to join with the National Day of Prayer event in Olympia, our state capital, on that day. All across our state, Christians gathered in homes, churches, town squares, parks, courthouses and at our capital to pray for our nation. During the time of prayer at the state capital, I had the privilege of giving a report about Operation Rolling Thunder, National Day of Prayer and the Global Day of Prayer. It was my responsibility to close the meeting.

About half way through the prayer event on the capitol steps, the weather began to move in. As we entered a time of prayer headed by leaders from the different spheres of society, it began to rain and the wind began to blow so hard that all of the speakers moved for shelter. I was left alone to close the meeting. In the distance, the faint rumble of thunder could be heard.

Sharon Eldridge of Pray Skagit served as the National Day of Prayer and Global Day of Prayer Coordinator for their state. Sharon shared that just before their National Day of Prayer they heard "rolling thunder," The thunder was mixed with hail, reminding her of Psalm 18:6-14.

We heard numerous reports from other coordinators and intercessors of thunderstorms that day. The weathermen reported about thunderstorms that stretched from our west coast to our eastern border in Washington. But this year, Operation Rolling Thunder went far beyond the borders of Washington.

2007 Results

Operation Rolling Thunder grew from 80+ churches in 10 cities in 2005, to 235+ churches in 2007. These churches engaged in 31 days of 24/7 prayer in 2006, and 1512 days in 2007.

- 513 days of 24/7 prayer occurred during the 24 day period between the National Day of Prayer and the Global Day of Prayer, while 999 days were committed to after the Global Day of Prayer.
- As of this year Washington State has 24/7 prayer offered up every day by some church or ministry.
- Churches in these counties followed ORT strategy:
  - Whatcom, Snohomish, King, Spokane, Thurston and Grays Harbor
- The city of Deer Park with Pastor Tim White had 3 churches commit to each taking one day per week of 24/7 prayer. This equates to 156 days of 24/7 prayer in their region.

In 2006 we had 70+ days of fasting, while in 2007 82,000+ days of fasting were committed to. Saints and churches joined us from Alabama, Nevada, California, New Jersey, Pakistan, Holland, Nigeria,

Uganda, Kenya, Rwanda, Sri Lanka, India and Israel. Many thanks go to Angela Greenig, of Set Free Ministries, who played a key role in mobilizing her network of 6,500 churches throughout Holland and Pakistan to join with us in prayer and fasting. Pastor Elistan Supeyo, of Joy Bringers International in Seattle, played an important role locally as well, mobilizing prayer and fasting among immigrants from Africa.

Pastor Stephen Thompson, of Victory Foursquare in Marysville, reported that during their day of 24/7 prayer a man who was blind in one eye walked in off the street. They prayed and God opened the man's eye. Pastor Thompson said that was the first time they had ever seen God heal an eye. He also said that for the last 30 days they had seen an unusual increase in salvations and healings.

Whatcom County CONECTer, Pastor Jason Hubbard, passed on a report from Pastor Jim, a city CONECTer in Blaine. The email said, "We have had five, let me say that again, five churches in the surrounding area that are coming together on a nightly basis moving in the Spirit of the Lord together. The greatest part is we are completely unified! Praise the Lord! We also baptized 7 people and had 4 salvations and lots of individuals give their hearts back to the Lord. Healings, oh my, we have had healings in backs, eyes, legs, arms, blood pressure and especially spiritual wounds."

King county led the state with the most prayer mobilized thanks to Pastor Gloria Locken, who oversaw the west side. A host of other city coordinators mobilized as well, resulting in 239 days of 24/7 prayer during ORT. Thurston county CONECTer Cynthia Rankin, Skagit county NDP Coordinator Sharon Eldridge, and Pastor Tim White in Deer Park, Spokane county all played major roles in mobilizing their respective areas.

Whatcom County CONECTer, Pastor Jason Hubbard, reported that Christ the King in Bellingham had mobilized enough people to pray that they were only 3 hours short on a weekly basis of having every day covered with 24/7 prayer. Combine this one large church with the 10 other local churches and 1 ministry who took at least one day and that equates to a large volume of prayer which covers his city, his county and our state. Thank you Lord!

The city of Renton CONECTer, Hank Mills, was in Spokane on the Global Day of Prayer and reported hearing radio hosts talking about how they had noted an increase in "rolling thunder."

There are so many more testimonies and people who could be mentioned. They deserve honor for the role they played. Truly, the body of Christ is arising as one man with one heart for One's glory; and that One is King Jesus. I have listed only a fraction of the testimonies that could be given and a fraction of the people who made tremendous contributions. It is my hope that by sharing just a few of the names, places, people and events we can understand that the strategy requires a huge number of people. As each person does their part, our Lord is glorified and His kingdom is extended. I thank God for each of you and especially for those who have not been mentioned. I know that your obedience and labor has been recorded in heaven.

Testimonies from the Transformation Task Force

The following testimonies represent some of the results of combining prayer with outreach into the 7 spheres of society. In order to be sensitive and not to draw undo attention to anyone, certain details have been omitted.

- A Key to Transforming a City - A mayor received Jesus Christ as his savior.

- Uncommon Teamwork – The Transformation Task Force connected a government official and a house of prayer to focus prayer on the tragic crime of human trafficking in their region. As a result an increase in trafficking related cases was brought to the attention of law enforcement (Romans 13:1-7), and an increase in awareness-raising events has occurred in the region. The goal of this strategic teamwork is targeted prayer in direct support of a Christian in government whose responsibility is to eradicate any form of human trafficking in our region. In essence, the result is that captives have been set free.

- Prayer on the floor of the House of Representatives - Direct ongoing prayer support was provided to a representative especially at times when they were on the floor of the House.

Revelation 5:13 ...."Blessing and honor and glory and power be to Him who sits on the throne, and to the Lamb, forever and ever!"

Chapter 12

The Strategy

The vision of our ministry is to declare and prepare. In the first eigchapterht chapters, I have declared to you the revelation God gave. Then I declared to you the history of Operation Rolling Thunder and the results of applying that revelation.

I am very passionate about putting faith in action. Operation Rolling Thunder provides a way for the Church to participate in restoring David's tabernacle and to gather the elders at the gates of a city while presenting the gospel of the kingdom. This chapter is designed to prepare you to unite with what God is doing through ORT so that your community might be transformed, through the presentation of the gospel of the kingdom.

The Simple Strategy

The strategy for Operation Rolling Thunder is very simple. It connects the leaders from every sphere of society who can help develop the most effective prayer and outreach strategies at that time. Simultaneously it unites corporate prayer and outreach events and ties them together through 24/7 prayer. Experience has proven many times that this has empowered local congregations to greatly increase the overall effectiveness of each prayer or outreach event. It also harnesses the momentum from these events to launch a long term campaign to transform communities.

The Two Primary Objectives

The first goal is to connect local strategic leaders representing all 7 spheres of society and position them to apply the principle of objective. This principle provides a systematic process that enables leaders to develop the very best strategy appropriate for their area. The second goal is to establish 24/7 prayer over a defined geographic area 365 days a year with a long term view to transform society through the presentation of the gospel of the kingdom.

The Bible says that in the last days God will restore David's fallen tabernacle. In following the pattern that God gave, we see that the leaders connected first at Hebron. Their purpose was to make one king.

The second goal is to set up 24/7 prayer, praise and worship in the City of David on Mount Zion. Then, under the canopy of continual prayer, the kingdom expanded on all fronts in every realm of society. We use the corporate prayer events to pray nationally and globally because there is tremendous power generated through the agreement in prayer. At the same time, wisdom says this is the perfect time to connect locally with other like-minded leaders from all the spheres of society. The goal is to drive responsibility and authority down to the lowest level possible. The Lord taught this to me through Matthew 4:17, which says, "Repent for the kingdom of heaven is at hand." So the question is, "What is in your hand?" What are you responsible for?

One of the first steps is to form a Transformation Task Force made up of leaders representing all 7 spheres of society. The key to deciding who should be on a specific task force will be determined by passion and geography. If you are a pastor and you are passionate about a city, then you need to develop relationship with kingdom-minded leaders from the other spheres of society who are passionate about your city. If you are a kingdom minded governor, then you need to be connected with other kingdom-minded leaders from the other spheres of society who are passionate about the same geography.

Role of the Transformation Task Force

I believe that a Transformation Task Force (TTF) can and should be formed in each local church, city, county, province, state, nation, and region. The TTF will accomplish a number of things:

- Identify catalysts in each sphere who have insight, strategy and authority.

- Apply Proverbs 24:5-6 and gather leaders at each regional level of influence. There is wisdom in a multitude of counsel, and by wise counsel you are to wage your own war.

- Provide critical spiritual intelligence to identify specific prayer targets in each area of responsibility.

- Help identify allies and their capabilities.

- Position leaders to develop the very best strategy, based upon a common objective and up to date spiritual intelligence.

- Create spiritual think   tanks.

Role of a CONECTer

A key role that must be filled is what I call a CONECTer. These people serve as the contact point for the leaders on the TTF, the watchmen or prophets, and intercessors.

Every church and region needs a CONECTer. You already know these people, and you probably call them a net-worker. I have found them in virtually every place I have visited. The training and equipping with the tools we provide through CONECT will provide each Transformation Task Force with their own centralized strategic communication center. This center links leaders from all 7 spheres with watchmen and intercessors to gather spiritual intelligence, as well as with mobilized mass concentrated prayer. CONECT also strengthens local congregations while providing their Transformation Task Force with up to date information. Thus the taskforce is equipped to make decisions based upon the most up to date spiritual intelligence. In addition, they are able to stay interconnected with the larger body of Christ.

The Strategy to Establish 24/7 Prayer in a City

The second goal in the pattern we saw was to establish 24/7 prayer. Most churches are too small to offer up 24/7 prayer 365 days a year. Ephesians 4:16 teaches us that when every part does their share it causes the body to edify itself in love. Any church can cover one day with 24/7 prayer. Therefore, if you can find 31 churches with each one willing to take one day, then your area can be covered with 24/7 prayer. I have found that leaders who catch the vision and are passionate about the presence of God will often commit their church to more than one day. The bottom line is cooperation, working together for a common purpose.

It is amazing what can be accomplished once the vision is caught and the strategy is understood. In 2009 for example, we saw congregations in Wasilla/Palmer Alaska under the direction of the Valley Pastor Prayer Network - Pastor Phil Markwardt president, and Kathy Conn, CONECTer - mobilize their community only one week before National Day of Prayer. Kansas State CONECTer, Donna Lippoldt, who headed up National Day of Prayer and the Family Policy Council, mobilized 216+ congregations in 16 cities in 4.5 months. She discovered that buying this book by the case and handing it out proved to be a powerful way to impart vision and equip cities to mobilize. I have great confidence that you also can mobilize your church or region quickly.

A Strategic Opportunity

If you understand the apostolic principles of war you will be equipped to see strategic opportunities. This is why I believe that every leader needs the training on the eight major biblical principles of war that we offer through our ministry.

Mass is one of principles. It defines combat power. This principle in Christian circles is often referred to as the power of agreement. The military teaches us that power can at times be determined by numbers of people. Leviticus 26:8 says that five will chase a 100 and 100 will chase 10,000. We understand from this that there is exponential power in prayer. Every person we add greatly increases our effectiveness.

This being the case on what day might my prayer have the greatest impact? Since I live in the US, that day is probably going to be the National Day of Prayer. Hence, if five million pray on that day then what a difference one more person will make! If one puts a thousand to flight and two ten thousand, well you do the math. It is huge! Therefore, I strongly urge you to take advantage of any major corporate prayer event, like the National Day of Prayer, Prayer Week, or the Global Day of Prayer, and join with them and their prayer strategy. It greatly increases the power the Church projects in prayer.

In 2009 we saw congregations in 24 nations use ORT to mobilize their communities. Many of these nations do not have a National Day of Prayer, but they have other events. Once you understand the principles and the strategy you can adapt it to fit your situation. For example we saw 23 churches in Lahore, Pakistan use ORT to launch regional prayer in August. 11 churches in Nairobi mobilized in November. A ministry on the University of Florida campus, called Unite Now, used the strategy to mobilize 14 ministries for a week of 24/7 prayer. Hakalay, Myanmar was the most recent village to be mobilized in December, 2009.

Praying Globally and Connecting Locally

The perfect opportunity to turn your attention towards your region is while you are gathered together with the body of Christ on a national or global level. You have mobilized your people and gathered the leaders. Why not leverage all this work and direct it towards a long-term campaign to transform your territory?

Occupation is a critical concept in transformation. In Luke 19:13 Jesus said, "Occupy till I come." Occupation is not an event. It is a long-term campaign just as Joshua and the children of Israel occupied the Promised Land. When David expanded the kingdom, they also occupied new territories.

There are two significant things I've learned in war. Air superiority is key to winning a war. But, the war will not be won until you get boots on the ground. You have got to occupy the land. Even if you defeat the enemy and win a piece of territory, if you do not occupy it, then the enemy can return and you will have to fight for it again. Mathew 12:43-45 teaches us a similar principle.

> *When an unclean spirit goes out of a man, he goes through dry places, seeking rest, and finds none. Then he says, 'I will return to my house from which I came.' And when he comes, he finds it empty, swept, and put in order. Then he goes and takes with him seven other spirits more wicked than himself, and they enter and dwell there; and the last state of that man is worse than the first. So shall it also be with this wicked generation.*

For the Church to secure the advances gained through major prayer and outreach campaigns, we have to be prepared to occupy the areas we take. We have to move from an event based mentality to a long term campaign mentality. This is where the wisdom of Ephesians 4:16 comes in. In order to occupy the mountain of prayer, we need to work together with each person, each congregation, and each ministry doing their share and standing their watch. This requires coordination and communication, in which a CONECTer plays a critical role. This is how we occupy the mountain of the Lord's house through 24/7/365 prayer.

> *Isaiah 2:2 Now it shall come to pass in the latter days That the mountain of the Lord 's house Shall be established on the top of the mountains, And shall be exalted above the hills; And all nations shall flow to it.*

The Transformation Task Force is way to mobilize your people to occupy the 7 mountains of   society. But, to be effective, they will need to move from focusing on an event to focusing on a long-term campaign. They need to get connected and stay connected. Communication, spiritual intelligence, teamwork, honor and the discipline to apply biblical principles of war are key elements in presenting the gospel of the kingdom in a long-term campaign.

There are also a number of key roles that need to be filled, trained and honored such as: CONECTers, Transformation Task Force Leaders, watchmen, prophets, intercessors, prayer leaders, outreach leaders, administrators and more.

The strategy for Operation Rolling Thunder can be used in any country at any time with any event. At this time, I am advocating that we connect with what Holy Spirit has orchestrated through the National Day of Prayer, Prayer Week and the Global Day of Prayer. God has orchestrated a tremendous crescendo of prayer around the world. This is a strategic time for you to impact not only your local area but also the world.

Two Phases

There are two phases in the ORT strategy. In Phase I the churches use corporate prayer events like National Day of Prayer and Global Day of Prayer to mobilize 24/7 prayer and form a Transformation Task Force. In Phase II, the Transformation Task Force and local churches implement a Chapter of CONECT to move from an event to a long term campaign in order to occupy their territory.

For complete details on resources, websites, the Spiritual War College, and CONECT see the appendix or visit www.ORTPrayer.org & www.KingdomLeague.org.

I will use 2008 as an example of how the strategy was employed. The only major changes to this strategy each year in the US are the dates. In other countries the major prayer events could be different. I strongly urge you to pray and obey what the Lord decrees for your region.

Phase I – 2008

The target dates for Phase corresponded to the National Day of Prayer (NDP), which fell on May 1, and the Global Day of Prayer (GDOP), which occurred on May 11. Prayer Week fell in between these two events.

- The Dates
  - May 1 – May 11
- The goals:
  - Host corporate prayer events on NDP and GDOP.
  - Establish 24/7 prayer during those dates, with 1 church taking responsibility for each day through ORT.
  - Form a Transformation Task Force, made up of leaders from the 7 spheres of society, to provide oversight to these events and to develop appropriate prayer targets and outreach strategies.
- The preparation
  - Select leaders from each of the 7 spheres to serve as a chair person in the TTF.
  - Select one leader to be trained as a CONECTer to serve the TTF and coordinate 24/7 prayer in ORT.

- o Train watchmen to help gather spiritual intelligence for the TTF.
  - o Select a date to host a Kick Off.
- The Kick Off event
  - o Present the vision and training for ORT, NDP, GDOP and any other corporate prayer event being used. Ideally, the kick off needs to occur as early as possible, though I have seen a community accomplish the goal in as little as 10 days.
- The Transformation Task Force is formed through a breakout session with each of the 7 spheres represented. The chair person for each sphere asks their group two questions. "What would transformation look like?" "How will transformation be measured?"
- Visit www.ORTPrayer.org & www.KingdomLeague.org for the Operation Rolling Thunder Kit, which contains 3 hours of training on How to Form a Transformation Task Force.
- The CONECTer coordinates with and supports NDP and GDOP Coordinators while mobilizing 24/7 prayer and gathering spiritual intelligence for the assigned territory.
  - o A report is compiled and presented to the TTF, which they use to seek God for the specific prayer and outreach strategies to be used in their area.
- On May 1, ORT, NDP and the prayer strategy for GDOP launch simultaneously.

Phase II

Phase II moves the church from an event to a long term campaign in order to transform the   community through the gospel of the kingdom. This is done by establishing a Chapter of CONECT in a church or region. This provides a strategic communication plan and structure to maintain cooperation, coordinate ongoing 24/7 prayer, and maintain and grow the Task Force while staying connected to the larger body of Christ. The Church is now empowered to reposition from being reactive to being proactive. This is critical to moving into offensive apostolic operations to occupy first the mountain of prayer and then the 7 mountains of society.

In 2008 and 2009, we watched a number of churches and ministries build their networks utilizing this strategy. For example, Pakistan saw 127+ churches in five cities mobilized and networked in the first year. Our national CONECTer in Kenya, Pastor Thomas, saw his network grow from one congregation to over 50 churches in 12 cities in 18 months. This kingdom strategy works even in the midst of persecution.

- See the appendix for how to start your Chapter of CONECT.

Chapter 13

Pastors – How ORT Can Serve You

On April 1, 2009 Dutch Sheets asked me to speak at his conference in Colorado Springs, "Awakening in Our Day; Reformation in our Life Time." This was a great privilege for me as Dr. C. Peter Wagner was in the audience. He did not know it, but he had played an important role in the results we were seeing through Operation Rolling Thunder. In 1994 a ministry passed on to him my first manuscript titled, *Biblical Principles and Strategies - the Art of Corporate Spiritual Warfare.* In this manuscript I had shared about the eight major principles of war, how they were biblically based and how they could be applied in spiritual warfare today. He graciously wrote back to me and basically said, "Nice theory but it was written in a vacuum." There was no evidence.

Since 1994, I've been on a mission to prove the revelation and word God gave to me. God used Dr. Wagner to challenge me. In the 90s and early 2000s I used these principles to equip leaders to affect churches, cities and events. In 2005, I got to test them in a state through Operation Rolling Thunder. At the conference in 2009, I was able to thank Dr. Wagner for his challenge to prove God's word. The testimonies in this book are a product of that challenge.

I shared with the audience that since 2001 I had read very few new books. When I wrote about the seven spheres of society I did not do it because I had read someone's book. I got it by revelation, but it did not surprise me that other ministers had written about the seven mind molders years earlier. It did not surprise me that Johnny Enlow and Lance Wallnau were teaching about the seven mountains because God's word says that God does nothing unless He reveals it to His servants the prophets. I shared this because there was such a powerful theme throughout this conference. Each minister's gift and topic were flowing together to give a fuller picture of God's counsel and wisdom. It was a good illustration of how the body works together when joined generationally and functionally.

In 2003 Dr. Joseph G. Mattera published a book called <u>Ruling in the Gates, Preparing the Church to Transform Cities</u>.1 He made some powerful statements in chapter 13, "Ten Things about the Gospel of the Kingdom." He says things such as the kingdom:

- Transcends all culture

- Administrates and unites all things

- Must produce servants

- Is first won in the spirit

All I can say to Dr. Mattera's conclusions is, "Amen!" The ORT strategy is a kingdom strategy. The 24 nations it served in 2009 proved that it transcends culture. The strategy unites the church, congregation by congregation, to lift a canopy of 24/7 prayer while gathering the leaders of a city so that they can discover God's prayer and action strategy for their area. The leaders' job is to administrate kingdom prayer and action to transform their community. I get excited as I see a new breed of servant leaders emerging in each place. I love the last item mentioned in Dr. Mattera's list, "It first must be won in the spirit."

Dr. Mattera says, "Prayer only works if you're in vertical harmony with God and horizontal unity with man.[2] The result of having vertical and horizontal harmony in the body of Christ is that the power of God is released for a whole region!" He goes on to say, "As God's people unite in love and join their faith together in prayer, the gospel of the kingdom of God will strike down demonic hosts and advertise the gospel with mighty power.[3]"

This describes the experience of the leaders who have utilized ORT to mobilize their church, cities, counties, states and nations. Here are just a few of the testimonies we have continued to record since this book was first published in January 2008.

- January 2008 - FBI reports that crime in every major city in Washington declines. Channel 7 News reports Seattle reaches a 40 year low in crime. Decreasing crime is a sign.

- National Day of Prayer events increased by 300% and Global Day of Prayer events increased by 600% in Washington State compared to where we started in 2005. A large jump occurred when we reached 24/7/365.

- Five city prayer centers were birthed between May and June 2008: Bellingham Washington – CONECTer Pastor Jason Hubbard; Kissi Kenya; CONECTer Pastor Thomas Okinyi; two prayer centers in Pakistan, and one in Myanmar. (Due to persecution the names of the CONECTers have been withheld.)

- More signs and wonders were reported by those who hosted events. For example, CONECTer Jenny McCoy from Tukwila reported a rainbow over their event. This is the second rainbow in 4 years.

Rainbow over Tukwila GDOP event 2008 – last day of Phase I of ORT

- December 2008 - The prayer center in Pakistan planted a church in a jail. I received a letter from the Punjab government and the jail superintendent indicating this was the first church planted in a prison in Pakistani history.

March 17, 2009
Undersea Volcanic Eruption

- By December 2008, congregations in 12 cities had been united all year long in 24/7/365 prayer.

- March 17 through March 22, 2009 we were invited by Apostle Don and Sherri Dodd, of Freedom in Christ, to present Operation Rolling Thunder to churches in North Pole/Fairbanks Alaska. This was marked by a volcanic eruption on the day we arrived on the other side of the International Date Line. The next day, during the breakout sessions in Fairbanks, an earthquake was recorded 4 miles from our location. On the day we left, Mt. Redoubt erupted within two hours of our departure. A 2003 prophetic word from Dutch Sheets and Chuck Pierce referencing Alaska as the Alpha and Omega state and the International Date Line tied these events together.

- On March 27 I received a report about a Muslim who was guarding prisoners in a jail. The prisoners were doing what they call the "Operation Rolling Thunder prayers." The report says the guard saw a bright light and saw Jesus come and sit with the prisoners. He knelt down, prayed in a language he did not know, and accepted Jesus. He went home, told his family, and they accepted Jesus. Then he returned to ask the prisoners if he could join their church. (Names withheld for security reasons.)

Thundersnow reported within 1 hour of speaking at Dutch's Conference

- May, 2009 was the first month that the churches in North Pole/Fairbanks mobilized for ORT. Under the direction of CONECTer Paulette Rahm, Prophet Sherri Dodd reported that 113 earthquakes were recorded setting a new record. As they stormed the heavens, God shook the earth. (Psalm 18:6-14) This volcanic activity is related to a prophetic word given   by Dutch Sheets and Chuck

Pierce on their 50-state tour in 2003.

- April 1, 2009 Dutch Sheets invited me to speak at the "Awakening in Our Day; Reformation in our Life Time" conference in Colorado Springs. During the presentation I shared how we saw thundersnow at our Kick Off in 2007. Within one hour CeCi Sheets showed us on her Blackberry that thundersnow has occurred in the area. In fact it occurred in four cities in the region.

- CONECTer Jason Hubbard from Bellingham invited us to minister to their Transformation Task Force leaders to prepare them to mobilize for ORT. On the day we arrived, a waterspout was recorded to have moved from the water to the docks and then back out to sea. The day after we left an earthquake was recorded.

- April 30 to May 4, 2009 - The Valley Pastor Prayer Network in Wasilla/Palmer Alaska, headed by Pastor Phil Markwardt, invited me to present ORT to their churches. *This is the first time we ever prayed specifically for a sign. We asked the Lord for it to warm up to 80 degrees.* CONECTer, Kathy Conn, agreed with us in prayer. An email was sent referencing the weather report after the training, noting that there were three record warm days, with the last day setting a 40 year high. Within two hours of my flight departure the temperature dropped 20 degrees back to normal.

- Kansas State CONECTer Donna Lippoldt began mobilizing her state in December 2008 and launched ORT in April, 2009. She reported:

- o 216+ churches in 16 cities started ORT in Phase I.

- o In Phase II 250+ churches in 9 cities chose to continue 24/7/365 prayer.

- o On the first day thunderstorms and rainbows were reported at some events.

- o Wichita's homicide rate went from three per month to zero the first month.

22 Degree Halo – by
Brenda Taylor May
31, 2009

- o Topeka police chief asked to see a 3% decline in property crime. In the first month there was a 15.4% decline.

- o A seven year drought was broken with more rain in one day than in the previous seven years.

- o Reports of remarkable unity and reconciliation with the First Nations were received.

- o Haskel Indian Nations University reported 75 new decisions for Christ, with salvations occurring weekly.

- o The nation's premier abortion clinic in Wichita closed permanently. This critical event occured on the last day of Phase I of ORT.

- On the last day of Phase I, May 31, 2009, a 22 degree circle halo was recorded over Washington State. This day was also the last day of   the Global Day of Prayer. On that day, for the first time in history, Christians in 220 nations participated in prayer.

- Three churches were planted in the first year by the first five city prayer centers birthed in May of 2008.

- On August 23, 2009 we received a report from our National CONECTer in Pakistan that 23 churches in Lahore had formed our fifth prayer center.

- Wasilla/Palmer Alaska CONECTer Kathy Conn helped mobilize her community in only one week. Combining their prayer with North Pole/Fairbanks over 400 days of 24/7 prayer were lifted up. She reported a remarkable reconciliation with the Natives, the Church and the Jewish community. Some events were marked dramatically at the end with thunder and lightning. "One Lord Sunday" set a record with 4,000 in attendance. Christians in the prison in Sutton participated in the 24/7 prayer strategy. An unusual water spout was caught on film. A prominent media figure in Anchorage repented publically for his criticism of conservative candidates' positions on moral issues.

- George Otis Jr. and the Sentinel Group created the first transformation video almost 10 years ago. One of the stories told about Alamonga, Guatemala where jails were shut down and their land became very fruitful as illustrated by the huge vegetables it produced.

- I received a report on October 2, 2009 from the Wasilla/Palmer CONECTer, Kathy Conn, stating that

Alaska had an abundant harvest as indicated by:

- Great moose season.

- Fish Creek, which had been closed to dip net fishing for 15 years, was re-opened

- The Alaska State Fair in Palmer recorded a number of world records broken with:

    o   A 125.9 pound cabbage

    o   A 79 and 82.5 pound rutabagas

    o   State records were broken with a 17 pound mushroom

- November 8, the Anchorage Daily News reported that gold production was the highest reported since the 1916 gold rush.

- October 6, 2009, Kansas State CONECTer Donna Lippoldt reported that an article in "Grass and Grain" on September 29, 2009 stated that they had a record harvest and that the grain elevators were full. They were asking Texas and Oklahoma to help them store their excess grain.

- November 18, 2009 - Pastor Daniel, our CONECTer from Lotoitok, Kenya, reported that a 1.5 year drought broke after churches united and mobilized to pray through ORT.

- As of December 2009, ORT has mobilized 6000+ churches, in 108 cities, in 24 nations. Conservatively these churches are lifting up over 8000+ days of 24/7 prayer throughout the year.

This is just a sampling of the kinds of testimonies we regularly receive. All glory and honor go to our Lord Jesus Christ because, as each congregation joins in, they help build His house of prayer for all nations. Operation Rolling Thunder is a strategy that unites leaders and congregations to establish 24/7/365 prayer in their region and to administrate the presentation of the gospel of the kingdom into all spheres of society in order to transform culture. What I hope you see through these testimonies is that:

1. The signs and measurable results that have followed me also follow others who carry the same message and who operate the strategy.

2. ORT is a strategy that empowers the local leaders to unite and mobilize those passionate about transforming a common geographic area.

3. This strategy helps leaders build and connect networks.

From Catholic to Charismatic – Pentecostal to Presbyterian

Ephesians 4:16 says that, when the whole body is joined together and every part does their share, it causes the body to edify itself in love. When people ask me who participates in ORT, I tell them that we have from Catholic to Charismatic and from Pentecostal to Presbyterian working with us. Does everyone participate? No! But those who have a kingdom mind set do. Operation Rolling Thunder is a strategy that harnesses momentum and helps local leaders launch a long term campaign to transform their communities through the presentation of the gospel of the kingdom of our Lord Jesus Christ.

Strategy Puts Faith into Action Corporately

Operation Rolling Thunder is not a ministry, but a strategy. It is a strategy that enables leaders to take the vision of the kingdom - 24/7/365 prayer, transformation and the 7 spheres of society - and to PUT THEIR FAITH INTO ACTION NOW. I like James. He says, "Show me your faith without your works and I'll show you my faith by what I do." ORT is a way to put your faith into action and to position people to occupy their assigned territory until Jesus returns.

This book was first published in January 2008. This chapter was written about two years later. My experience has only strengthened my conviction concerning the gift God has given me and the effectiveness of the strategies and apostolic principles of war that He has taught me. Pastor, it is my sincerest desire to see you, your congregation and your city blessed and fulfilling the destiny God has planned for you. The principles and strategies God has given through ORT have now been utilized to mobilize and connect the body of Christ in 24 nations.

It is my sincerest prayer that the strategy my Father gave me will help you fulfill the vision and assignment God has given you, your congregation, and the Church in your city.

Appendix A

Resources

Operation Rolling Thunder – www.ORTPrayer.org & www.KingdomLeague.org

WMI's Spiritual War College – This War College provides advanced training for leaders on biblical principles of war and apostolic strategy. Every leader on a Transformation Task Force will benefit. Training is provided to Certify CONECTers and advanced trainings for watchmen/prophets and intercessors are also provided.

Chapter of CONECT – www.ORTPrayer.org & www.KingdomLeague.org

National Day of Prayer -

http://www.ndptf.org/home/index.cfm?flash=1

Prayer Week - http://www.i61.org/prayerweek/Home.html

Global Day of Prayer - http://www.globaldayofprayer.com/

Global Day of Prayer USA - http://www.gdopusa.com/

CD's & Books available from www.ORTPrayer.org & www.KingdomLeague.org

Appendix B

Chapter of CONECT

Chuck Pierce published a book in 2001 called <u>The Future War of the Church</u> (published by Regal Books from Gospel Lighthouse Ventura CA, USA) in which he lists several key things the church should do or be aware of (pages 21-23).

1. God is searching for those with a heart to lead troops.
2. We must think prophetically.
3. God is restoring the watchman anointing.
4. Watch your boundaries.
5. We must know how to communicate with each other immediately.
6. We must allow the Lord to teach us how to have a strong defense.
7. Communication is vital.

Page 87 – God says, "I need a government to demonstrate My purposes on Earth anew. I need an army who will come forth to break up the enemy's strategies and display My will on Earth. I need a government that takes what has been scattered and gathers it together to advance My kingdom."

CONECT provides a way to DO everything the prophet has declared the church needs to do. God is mobilizing an army for war. He used the military as part of my preparation for this season. I served on the admiral's staff who oversaw Desert Storm. While in the reserves, I served as the Executive Officer of a communication unit responsible for 1/4 of the Navy's communication. I also served as the Executive Officer of a   mobilization unit. I attended a course at the Navy War College, and served as a training officer for 7 years. God has prepared me with strategy, training and experience that are not available through any seminary or bible college.

The training delivered through our Spiritual War College is implemented through the Christian Outreach Network Establishing Church-wide Teamwork, otherwise known as CONECT. CONECT empowers the church to establish communication, disciplines and processes that enable spiritual catalysts to develop strategy specific to their area. At the same time, these catalysts mobilize the body of Christ to build the wall of prayer, family by family. They set a watch, connect kingdom minded churches, and provide tools and training for leaders, watchmen, and intercessors. The strategy can be applied to larger and larger geographic areas because biblical principles work regardless of the size. Hence, the acronym stands for either the Christian Outreach Network Establishing "City-wide Teamwork," or "County-wide Teamwork" or "Country-wide Teamwork."

I hope I can communicate this effectively. The solution is not technology. All technology does is automate or support a process. The key is to follow the disciplined processes that are biblically based. That is how CONECT empowers leaders to function like admirals, generals or an apostles. It is our intent to use the best technology available, but to never forget that technology is merely a tool that supports a process. This is why CONECT works well even in developing nations where technology is limited or non-existent.

CONECT drives responsibility and authority down to the lowest level possible. It will engage every family in your congregation while building the wall of prayer based upon your local ministry's vision. It helps leaders identify their   watchmen and facilitates the establishment of a watch. Simultaneously it trains one to serve as the leadership's CONECTer. It is based upon the apostolic model found in Nehemiah.

A Chapter of CONECT is formed when the leadership of the local church or a Transformation Task Force (TTF) select someone to be trained and serve as their CONECTer. They agree that their purpose is to establish the gospel of the kingdom in their territory in all 7 spheres of society. They agree to follow certain communication processes, protocols and disciplines that facilitate good teamwork and coordination for the purpose of advancing the kingdom. The Chapter of CONECT enables a TTF or a church to maintain their unique identity and authority, while acknowledging they are an inter-dependent part of a larger body. Each individual wants to be connected to other kingdom minded leaders and organizations so they can cooperatively advance the kingdom in their respective territories.

For more information go to www.ORTPrayer.org & www.KingdomLeague.org and order or download the booklet "How to Establish a Chapter of CONECT." It contains all the requirements and forms.

Appendix C

Definitions of Roles

Transformation Task Force (TTF) – A TTF is made up of 7 apostolic councils with a chairperson serving over each council. These councils gather spiritual catalysts to discover key prayer and action strategies to be launched during Operation Rolling Thunder in support of a long term goal to transform their communities through the presentation of the gospel of the kingdom. They work directly with a CONECTer. See appendix A and B.

7 Spheres of Society – Church, business, government, media, education, healthcare and the family. Note that the church represents religion as well.

Chairperson – A chairperson is required for each council to facilitate their meetings. Over time, specific gifts will be recognized and proven. Those with apostolic and prophetic gifts become evident. Eventually one who functions with the fruit of an apostle will be the chairperson.

CONECTer – This a person who serves the Transformation Task Force (TTF), whether that be in a church, the TTF in a city, the TTF in a county or the TTF in a nation, . They are the primary point of communication and connection with leaders, watchmen, intercessors, and other TTF's. They serve their leadership team just like Hananiah the captain of the citadel served Nehemiah. They manage the watch, receive reports from watchmen, prepare reports for their leadership team, and manage the 24/7 prayer. They also recruit and train other CONECTers to serve the network that grows through their TTF.

Watchman –Prophets, people with a prophetic gift and those who are part of the 24/7 watch and who have been trained in the CONECT strategy and reporting process. They work closely with the TTF and other CONECTers to glean spiritual intelligence through prayer, research and prayer walking. They participate in the 24/7 watch and work closely with the CONECTer who manages the watch.

Intercessor – Everyone is an intercessor. Intercession occurs when someone prays on behalf of another person. In the Navy, there were certain times when we had to gather "all hands on deck." During corporate prayer events like National Day of Prayer, Prayer Week, and Global Day of Prayer every person ought to gather to pray and intercede due to the exponential power that is added through each person. If you a pastor, minister, or a five-fold leader, then I challenge you to mobilize your whole congregation or ministry during these strategic "all hands on deck" times.

Coordinator – These are important temporary volunteer positions that oversee a specific event or an area. They perform functions similar to a CONECTer. One of the primary differences between a CONECTer and a Coordinator is that the CONECTer also oversees 24/7/365 prayer and recruits coordinators for the events their TTF determines they want to participate in. The CONECTer performs their function year round, while the Coordinator's function is centered on one event.

Appendix D

24/7 Prayer Strategies and Resources

Moravians – 24 men and 24 women each committing to one hour per day started the 100 year prayer vigil.

International House of Prayer – Kansas City – 24/7 PPW one location

One Church takes responsibility for each day of the week or month.

- 7 churches working together can cover their region with 24/7/365 prayer if each church commits to one day per week.
- 31 churches working together can cover their region with 24/7/365 prayer if each church commits to one day per month.

1 person praying 24 hours

2 people each taking 12 hours

3 people each taking 8 hours

4 people each taking 6 hours

6 people each taking 4 hours

8 people each taking 3 hours

12 people each taking 2 hours

24 people each taking 1 hour

Pray in together one location.

Pray in homes.

Remember, every person we add exponentially increases the power in the prayer.

The CONECTer is the key that joins these praying people to the Transformation Task Force. CONECT provides all the training, tools and processes to empower local churches to mobilize every single family to build the wall of prayer. The same principles, tools and processes apply to your city, your county, your state and nation.

End Notes

Chapter 1

1   Dutch Sheets cited in Eddie L. Lawrence, D. Min., "The Forerunner Anointing," (First Breath Ministries, Killen Alabama, 2005) p. 5.

Chapter 2

1   OT:8403 tyn!b=T^ tabniyth (tab-neeth'); from OT:1129; structure; by implication, a model, resemblance: KJV - figure, form, likeness, pattern, similitude. (Biblesoft's New Exhaustive Strong's Numbers and Concordance with Expanded Greek-Hebrew Dictionary. Copyright © 1994, 2003 Biblesoft, Inc. and International Bible Translators, Inc.)

2   Tim Taylor, "Biblical Principles and Strategies the Art of Corporate Spiritual Warfare," (Watchman Ministries International, Renton, Washington, 2003) p. 15.

3   Tim Taylor, "Biblical Principles and Strategies the Art of Corporate Spiritual Warfare," (Watchman Ministries International, Renton, Washington, 2003) p. 40.

4   OT:2275 Chebrown (kheb-rone'); from OT:2267; seat of association; Chebron, a place in Palestine, also the name of two Israelites: KJV - Hebron. (Biblesoft's New Exhaustive Strong's Numbers and Concordance with Expanded Greek-Hebrew Dictionary. Copyright © 1994, 2003 Biblesoft, Inc. and International Bible Translators, Inc.)

5   Modern Language Association (MLA): "association." Dictionary.com Unabridged (v 1.1). Random House, Inc. 14

Nov. 2007. <Dictionary.com
http://dictionary.reference.com/browse/association>.

Chapter 3

1   OT:3427 bv^y* yashab (yaw-shab'); a primitive root; properly,
    to sit down (specifically as judge. in ambush, in quiet); by
    implication, to dwell, to remain; causatively, to settle, to marry:
    KJV - (make to) abide (-ing), continue, (cause to, make to)
    dwell (-ing), easeself, endure, establish, fail, habitation, haunt,
    (make to) inhabit (-ant), make to keep [house], lurking, marry (-
    ing), (bring again to) place, remain, return, seat, set (-tle),
    (down-) sit (-down, still, -ting down, -ting [place] -uate), take,
    tarry. (Biblesoft's New Exhaustive Strong's Numbers and
    Concordance with Expanded Greek-Hebrew Dictionary.
    Copyright © 1994, 2003 Biblesoft, Inc. and International Bible
    Translators, Inc.)

2   Rick Joiner, "Epic Battles of the Last Days," (Morningstar
    Publications, Charlotte, NC, 1995) p. 20.

3   Al Houghton, "The Sure Mercies of David," (Word at Work
    Ministries Inc., Placentia, California, 2007) pp. 13-14.

Chapter 4

1   Bill Johnson, "The Supernatural Power of a Transformed
    Mind," (Destiny Image Publishers, Inc. Shippensburg, PA,
    2005) p. 43.

2   Bill Johnson, "The Supernatural Power of a Transformed
    Mind," (Destiny Image Publishers, Inc. Shippensburg, PA,
    2005) p. 51.

Chapter 5

1   See Appendix A for teaching and training regarding biblical principles of war.

2   See Appendix A, B and C for training, resources and information regarding CONECT.

3   Tellis A. Bethel, "America, A Destiny Unveiled," (Xulon Press, 2003) pp. 62-63.

4   Tim Taylor, "Biblical Principles and Strategies the Art of Corporate Spiritual Warfare," (Watchman Ministries International, Renton, Washington, 2003) p. 67.

Chapter 6

1   Barbara Wentroble, "Prophetic Intercession," (Renew Books a Division of Gospel Lighthouse, Ventura California, USA, 1999) p. 128.

2   Chuck Pierce, Dutch Sheets, recorded and transcribed from CD, December 14-15, 2003 at Sonrise Chapel, Everett, Washington on 50 state tour.

3   See Appendix A, B and C for training, resources and information regarding CONECT.

4   NT:4592 semeion (say-mi'-on); neuter of a presumed derivative of the base of NT:4591; an indication, especially ceremonially or supernaturally: KJV - miracle, sign, token, wonder. (Biblesoft's New Exhaustive Strong's Numbers and Concordance with Expanded Greek-Hebrew Dictionary. Copyright © 1994, 2003 Biblesoft, Inc. and International Bible Translators, Inc.)

5   *Holy Bible, New Living Translation ®, copyright © 1996, 2004 by Tyndale Charitable Trust. Used by permission of Tyndale House Publishers. All rights reserved.*

Chapter 7

1   Jack Frost, "Experiencing Father's Embrace," (Destiny Image
      Publishers, Inc., Shippensburg, PA, 2002) p. 103.

Chapter 8

1   Modern Language Association (MLA): "Catalysts." The
      American Heritage® Dictionary of the English Language,
      Fourth Edition. Houghton Mifflin Company, 2004. 14 Nov.
      2007. <Dictionary.com
      http://dictionary.reference.com/browse/Catalysts>.

2   Genesis 22:14

3   Tim Taylor, "Biblical Principles and Strategies the Art of
      Corporate Spiritual Warfare," (Watchman Ministries
      International, Renton, Washington, 2003) p. 15.

4   NT:4754 strateuomai (strat-yoo'-om-ahee); middle voice from
      the base of NT:4756; to serve in a military campaign;
      figuratively, to execute the apostolate (with its arduous duties
      and functions), to contend with carnal inclinations: KJV -
      soldier, (go to) war (-fare). (Biblesoft's New Exhaustive
      Strong's Numbers and Concordance with Expanded Greek-
      Hebrew Dictionary. Copyright © 1994, 2003 Biblesoft, Inc.
      and International Bible Translators, Inc.)

5   Tim Taylor, "Biblical Principles and Strategies the Art of
      Corporate Spiritual Warfare," (Watchman Ministries
      International, Renton, Washington, 2003) p. 27.

6   NT:4752 strateia (strat-i'-ah); from NT:4754; military service,
      i.e. (figuratively) the apostolic career (as one of hardship and
      danger): KJV - warfare. (Biblesoft's New Exhaustive Strong's
      Numbers and Concordance with Expanded Greek-Hebrew

Dictionary. Copyright © 1994, 2003 Biblesoft, Inc. and International Bible Translators, Inc.)

7   C. Peter Wagner, "Apostles Prophets and the Foundation of the Church," (Regal Books a Division of Gospel Light, Ventura California, USA, 2000) p. 37.

8   See Appendix A for WMI's Spiritual War College training.

9   Modern Language Association (MLA): "transform." Dictionary.com Unabridged (v 1.1). Random House, Inc. 14 Nov. 2007. <Dictionary.com http://dictionary.reference.com/browse/transform>.

10   Modern Language Association (MLA): "task." Dictionary.com Unabridged (v 1.1). Random House, Inc. 14 Nov. 2007. <Dictionary.com http://dictionary.reference.com/browse/task>.

11   Modern Language Association (MLA): "force." Dictionary.com Unabridged (v 1.1). Random House, Inc. 14 Nov. 2007. <Dictionary.com http://dictionary.reference.com/browse/force>.

Chapter 9

1   See Appendix A for the National Day of Prayer website.

2   See Appendix A for the Global Day of Prayer website.

3   See Appendix A for Prayer Week's website.

4   See Appendix A and B for training, resources and information regarding WMI's Spiritual War College courses and CONECT.

5   See <www.ORTPrayer.org & www.KingdomLeague.org> for
     pictures of signs and wonders such as the rainbow, circum-
     horizon arc or the sun.

6   See <www.ORTPrayer.org & www.KingdomLeague.org> or
     <www.CONECT.US> for pictures of signs and wonders such
     as the rainbow, circum-horizon arc or the sun.

7   Media contact Carmeyia Gillis, NOAA Space Environment
     Center , "NOAA Issues Space Weather Warning," accessed
     May 16, 2005, <
     http://www.noaanews.noaa.gov/stories2005/s2437.htm>

8   Diane Fink provided the notes she used during the "Piercing
     the Heavens Conference" October 2005 presented at Sonrise
     Chapel in Everett Washington.

Chapter 10

1   See Appendix A, B and C for training, resources and
     information regarding CONECT.

2   See Appendix C for information regarding a Transformation
     Task Force.

3   See Appendix C for a definition of the days of prayer.

4   See <www.ORTPrayer.org & www.KingdomLeague.org> or
     <www.CONECT.US> for pictures of signs and wonders such
     as the rainbow, circum-horizon arc or the sun.

5   *The Daily Mail,* "A Rainbow of Fire Observed in the
     Northwest" (June 11, 2006). It can also be viewed online at
     <http://en.wikipedia.org/wiki/Circumhorizontal_arc >

6   Office of the Washington State Climatologist, "Washington 2006 Top 10 Weather & Climate Events," accessed September 2007, http://www.climate.washington.edu/events/2006top10.html

7   Office of the Washington State Climatologist, "Washington 2006 Top 10 Weather & Climate Events," accessed September 2007, http://www.climate.washington.edu/events/2006top10.html

8   Prophecy JERUSALEM FLOODS ON 40 YEAR ANNIVERSARY--THE CITY IS TARGETED FOR A HOLY SPIRIT INVASION! Chuck Pierce : May 19, 2007 Glory of Zion Ministries <http://www.lightthehighway.org/en/index.php/Jerusalem_Floods_-_Chuck_Pierce_-_05.19.07>

9   PUBLIC INFORMATION STATEMENT NATIONAL WEATHER SERVICE SEATTLE WA 200 PM PST THU DEC 21 2006

10 NT: 4592 semeion (say-mi'-on); neuter of a presumed derivative of the base of NT:4591; an indication, especially ceremonially or supernaturally: KJV - miracle, sign, token, wonder. (Biblesoft's New Exhaustive Strong's Numbers and Concordance with Expanded Greek-Hebrew Dictionary. Copyright © 1994, 2003 Biblesoft, Inc. and International Bible Translators, Inc. and Englishman's Concordance.)

11 See Appendix C for a definition of a Transformation Task Force.

12 See Appendix C for a definition and role of a CONECTer.

13 Office of the Washington State Climatologist, "Washington 2006 Top 10 Weather & Climate Events," accessed September 2007, http://www.climate.washington.edu/events/2006top10.html

14 Thundersnow also known as a Winter Thunderstorm or a Thunder Snowstorm is a particularly rare meteorological phenomenon that includes the typical behavior of a thunderstorm, but with snow falling as the primary precipitation instead of rain. It commonly falls in regions of strong upward motion within the cold sector of extratropical cyclones between autumn and spring when surface temperatures are most likely to be near or below freezing. Variations exist, such as thundersleet, where the precipitation consists of sleet rather than snow. Wikapedia.com accessed September 2007.
<http://en.wikipedia.org/wiki/Thundersnow> >

15 Lynda V. Mapes, Seattle Times staff reporter, "The eagles are landing in record numbers."

Chapter 11

1 Thundersnow, Wikapedia.com, accessed September 2007.
<http://en.wikipedia.org/wiki/Thundersnow> >

2 See Appendix B for information regarding a Chapter of CONECT.

3 See Appendix A, B and C for information regarding a Chapter of CONECT.

4 Personal phone interview with Pastor Thompson, Victory Foursquare in Marysville, WA, June 2007.

5 Email received from Pastor Jason Hubbard May 26, 2007 with report from Pastor Jim the CONECTer for Blaine in Operation Rolling Thunder.

6 Reuters News Service, "No Housing Woes in Booming Washington State," San Francisco, Filed 11:10 a.m. ET September 20, 2007.

Chapter 12

1   Romans 8:19

2   See Appendix C for a definition of Operation Rolling Thunder and resources.

3   See Appendix C for a definition of a Transformation Task Force and resources.

4   See Appendix C for a definition of CONECTer and see Appendix A and B for CONECTer resources.

5   See Appendix D for 24/7 prayer strategies and resources.

Chapter 13

1-3. Dr. Joseph G. Mattera, "Ruling in the Gates, Preparing the Church to Transform Cities," Creation House Press © 2003, Chapter 13, pg. 76, pg. 78

For more information about Kingdom League International, Operation Rolling Thunder, CONECT, the Spiritual War College, or to invite Tim to speak please write, email or visit the website:

Kingdom League International

4004 NE 4th Street, Suite 107-350

Renton, WA 98056

(425) 687-0994

Email Admin@KingdomLeauge.org

www.ORTPrayer.org

www.KingdomLeague.org